Essential
Australia

by Anne Matthews

PASSPORT BOOKS

NTC/Contemporary Publishing Group

Above: *lifeguard on famous Bondi Beach*

Front cover: *Ayers Rock; Sydney Opera House; koala*
Back cover: *Aboriginal art*

This edition first published in 2000 by Passport Books, a division of NTC/ Contemporary Publishing Group, Inc. 4255 West Touhy Avenue, Lincolnwood (Chicago), Illinois 60712–1975 U.S.A.

Revised second edition 2000
Copyright © 1998 The Automobile Association 1998; © 2000 The Automobile Association and Periplus Editions
Maps © 2000 Periplus Editions

The contents of this publication are believed correct at the time of printing. Nevertheless, the publishers cannot accept responsibility for errors or omissions, nor for changes in details given. We are always grateful to readers who let us know of any errors or omissions they come across, and future printings will be updated accordingly.

Published by Passport Books in conjunction with The Automobile Association of Great Britain.

Written by Anne Matthews

Library of Congress Catalog Card Number: on file
ISBN 0-658-00377-1

Color separation: BTB Digital Imaging, Whitchurch, Hampshire

Printed and bound in Italy by Printer Trento srl

The weather chart on **page 118** of this book is calibrated in °C. For conversion to °F simply use the following formula:

$$°F = 1.8 \times °C + 32$$

Contents

About this Book 4

Viewing Australia 5–14
Anne Matthews' Australia 6
Australia's Features 7
Essence of Australia 8–9
The Shaping of Australia 10–11
Natural Australia 12–13
Australia's Famous 14

Top Ten 15–26
Cairns and District 16
The Gold Coast 17
The Great Barrier Reef 18–19
Great Ocean Road 20
Kakadu National Park 21
The Kimberley 22
Blue Mountains 23
Sydney Harbour and
Sydney Opera House 24
Tasmania's World Heritage Area 25
Uluru-Kata Tjuta National Park 26

What To See 27–90
New South Wales 30–43
Food and Drink 44–5
Queensland 47–55
Victoria and Tasmania 57–67
In the Know 68–9
South Australia and Northern
Territory 71–81
Western Australia 83–90

Where To... 91–116
Eat and Drink 92–9
Stay 100–3
Shop 104–9
Take Children 110–11
Be Entertained 112–16

Practical Matters 117–24

Index 125–6

Acknowledgments 126

About this Book

Essential *Australia* is divided into five sections to cover the most important aspects of your visit to Australia.

Viewing Australia pages 5–14
An introduction to Australia by the author.
  Australia's Features
  Essence of Australia
  The Shaping of Australia
  Peace and Quiet
  Australia's Famous

Top Ten pages 15–26
  The author's choice of the Top Ten places to visit in Australia, each with practical information.

What to See pages 27–90
The five main areas of Australia, each with its own brief introduction and an alphabetical listing of the main attractions.
  Practical information
  Snippets of 'Did You Know...' information
  3 suggested walks
  4 suggested tours
  2 features

Where To... pages 91–116
The best places to eat, stay, shop, take children and be entertained.

Practical Matters pages 117–24
A highly visual section containing essential travel information.

Maps
All map references are to the individual maps found in the What to See section of this guide.
For example, Sydney Harbour Bridge has the reference ➕ 32B5 – indicating the page on which the map is located and the grid square in which bridge is to be found. A list of the maps that have been used in this travel guide can be found in the index.

Prices
Where appropriate, an indication of the cost of an establishment is given by **$** signs:
$$$** denotes higher prices, **$$** denotes average prices, while **$ denotes lower charges.

Star Ratings
Most of the places described in this book have been given a separate rating:
✪✪✪ Do not miss
✪✪ Highly recommended
✪ Worth seeing

Viewing
Australia

Anne Matthews' Australia   6
Australia's Features   7
Essence of Australia   8–9
The Shaping of Australia   10–11
Natural Australia   12–13
Australia's Famous   14

Above: *A young surfer*
Right: *A cuddly koala*

5

Anne Matthews'
Australia

Discovery and Settlement

For centuries man believed in the existence of some great southern landmass, but it was not until the 17th century that European seafarers sighted Australia's western coast. Then, in 1770, James Cook discovered the continent's east coast, and eighteen years later the first reluctant 'settlers' – British convicts and soldiers – arrived to disrupt the isolated existence of the Aboriginal people who had lived here for over 50,000 years.

From its unpromising convict beginnings, Australia has developed into a wealthy and politically stable nation of over 18 million people. Since the early days of dependence on Britain, the national self-esteem has grown decade by decade for the past 200 or so years, and Australia will showcase its confidence and vibrancy to the world at the 2000 Olympic Games.

Although proud of its pioneering history and Outback traditions, this is the world's most urbanized society, with 88 per cent of the population living in towns and cities. Most of these settlements are around the coast – far away from the vast and inhospitable interior that takes up a large percentage of the continent's area.

Australia – variously known as 'Down Under', 'Oz', and the 'best address on earth' – is vast: approximately 24 times the size of the British Isles and as big as continental USA (without Alaska). The terrain and climate obviously vary considerably, but overall the weather is warm and sunny, and the scenery varies from interesting to magnificent.

This benign climate has undoubtedly affected the Australian character, best described as egalitarian and relaxed. Aussies are friendly and laid-back, and visitors from everywhere are welcomed

Many ancient Aboriginal rock art sites are scattered throughout the continent

enthusiastically. This is a successfully multicultural nation where, despite some intolerance towards Aborigines in particular, people of European, Asian, Arabic, Pacific Island and other origins live together in relative harmony.

Visitors should remember that Australia is enormous – it is over 4,000km from Sydney to Perth – so unless you have months to spare, select your destinations carefully.

Sydney's famous Opera House, completed in 1973, is an unmistakable symbol of Australia's largest city

Australia's Features

Natural Features
• Australia is the world's smallest and flattest continent and, after Antarctica, the driest.
• Australia's coastline is an incredible 36,700km.
• Australia's highest point is Mount Kosciuszko in southern New South Wales – a mere 2,228m high. The lowest point is 16m below sea level at Lake Eyre in Outback South Australia.
• The Great Barrier Reef is the world's largest living, growing structure – it is composed primarily of coral polyps and algae, and stretches for over 2,000km along the Queensland coast.

Make-up and People
• Australia is made up of six states – New South Wales, Queensland, Victoria, Tasmania, South Australia and Western Australia; two territories – the Australian Capital Territory (the location of Canberra, the national capital) and the Northern Territory; and external territories, including Norfolk Island and Christmas Island.
• Although of a similar size to the United States (population over 250 million), and 24 times the size of Britain, Australia is home to just 18.3 million people. The population of Sydney, the largest city, is 3.8 million.
• Over 77,000 migrants arrived in Australia in 1997–8. Of these, 14,700 people came from New Zealand, 9,200 from Britain, and 4,300 from China.

The modernistic architecture of Darling Harbour frames some of Sydney's tallest buildings

Road and Rail
• Australia has more than 810,000km of roads, but only 35 per cent are sealed with bitumen or concrete.
• The world's longest straight stretch of railway is in Outback Western Australia – it is 478.4km long.

Odds and Ends
• Although shark attacks do occur, fewer than 100 people have been killed by these creatures since 1791.
• Australia's highest recorded temperature is 53.1°C, measured at Cloncurry in Queensland in January 1889.
• Between 1788 and 1856, 157,000 convicts were transported to Australia.
• Surveys have revealed that Australia's top tourist attraction is Sydney's shopping.

Essence of Australia

Bottom: A visit to Uluru (Ayers Rock) is an essential of any trip to Australia

Australia's warm climate is perfect for all types of sporting activity

Visitors come to Australia for many reasons, but the continent's greatest appeal is undoubtedly its 'Great Outdoors'. The climate is generally warm and balmy, the magnificent scenery includes rugged sandstone peaks and escarpments, rainforests, gleaming white sands and clear tropical waters, and the unique plants, birds and animals add an exotic touch to an already dramatic landscape.

There are also many historical and cultural experiences to be savored in Australia. The locals are friendly, warm and welcoming, and this relaxed atmosphere is complemented by fabulous food and wine. A visit 'Down Under' may well surprise you with its variety of experiences.

THE **10** ESSENTIALS

If you have only a short time to visit Australia and would like to sample the very best that the continent has to offer, here are the essentials:

Dining out, especially alfresco, is enormously popular with visitors and locals alike

• **Take a cruise on Sydney Harbour** (➤ 24) and enjoy the beautiful scenery at the heart of Australia's most famous city.

• **Spend a day at the beach** to experience the sun, surf and sheer hedonism of Bondi (➤ 31) or any other of Australia's magnificent beaches. You could even have a go at surfing.

• **See a performance at the Sydney Opera House,** where you can enjoy the acclaimed Australian Ballet, Australian Opera or Sydney Symphony Orchestra inside the nation's most distinctive building (➤ 24).

• **Experience the Great Barrier Reef** – snorkel or dive among the colorful coral and luminously colored fish of the eighth wonder of the world (➤ 18–19).

• **Dine alfresco** to sample modern Australian cuisine, especially some of the wonderful seafood, at an outdoor table with a view across the water.

• **Visit Uluru (Ayers Rock)** – at the very heart of the continent, the world's largest monolith exudes an awesome sense of mystery and timelessness (➤ 26).

• **Learn about Australia's history** – discover something of pre-European Aboriginal life at the Australian Museum

(➤ 34), and head to Port Arthur (➤ 67) for an insight into the harsh convict days.

• **Go bushwalking** – a hike in the bush (countryside) is a must. Explore the escarpments and eucalypt forests of the Blue Mountains (➤ 23, 41).

• **Visit a wildlife park** for a close encounter with kangaroos, emus, wombats, koalas and other unique Australian fauna (➤ 35).

• **Sample local wines and beers** – spend an evening in an Aussie pub, meet the locals, and enjoy world-class wines and fine beers.

Enjoy Australia's 'Great Outdoors', but remember to protect yourself from the fierce sun

The Shaping of Australia

James Cook and the crew of the Endeavour *at Botany Bay in 1770*

1779
In England, following the cessation of convict transportation to America in 1776, the first suggestions are made that New South Wales could become a penal colony.

40,000–50,000 years ago
Aborigines arrive in Australia from what is now Southeast Asia.

1606
Dutch explorer Willem Jansz sails past the Queensland coast, proving that what is known as *Terra Australis Incognita* does exist.

1770
Lieutenant James Cook and the *Endeavour* crew land at Botany Bay, south of Sydney, and later claim the eastern coast of New Holland (Australia) for King George III, under the name of New South Wales.

1787
The 'First Fleet' departs from England on 13 May to sail to Botany Bay. The fleet's 11 ships carry over 1,400 people, among whom are 759 male and female convicts.

1788
The Fleet arrives in Botany Bay on 20 January. The Fleet's commander and first Governor of the colony, Captain Arthur Phillip, decides the site is unsuitable and on 26 January moves north to Port Jackson (Sydney Harbour). The colony of New South Wales is proclaimed.

1790
The Second Fleet, with a

further 1,006 convicts, arrives.

1793
The first free settlers land in Sydney.

1804
Australia's second major colony is founded at Hobart, Tasmania.

1810
Scotsman Lachlan Macquarie becomes Governor and remains until 1821. During his stay, he transforms the unruly colony into a settlement with great potential and the population reaches 10,000.

1817
Governor Macquarie first refers to the colony as 'Australia' in official correspondence.

1824
Brisbane, the capital of Queensland, is founded.

1828
The first census reveals a population of 36,000 convicts and free settlers, and 2,549 military personnel.

1829
Perth and Fremantle are founded and Western Australia is proclaimed a British colony.

1832
Assisted emigration

begins – during the next 20 years over 200,000 people emigrate, mostly from Britain.

1835
The city of Melbourne is founded.

1836
The first settlers arrive in Adelaide, South Australia.

1840
Convict transportation to New South Wales ceases. A total of 83,000 convicts had been sent to the colony since 1788.

1859
Queensland, previously part of New South Wales, becomes a separate colony.

1869
Darwin, capital of the remote Northern Territory, is founded.

1901
The Commonwealth of Australia is proclaimed on 1 January, joining the six Australian colonies into a federation. Edmund Barton is elected as the first Prime Minister.

1908
Canberra is chosen as the site for the new national capital.

1923
Work begins on the construction of the Sydney Harbour Bridge, which is finally opened in 1932.

1927
The seat of national government moves from Melbourne to Canberra.

1947
Post-war immigration from Europe begins, starting the nation's slow but inexorable surge towards multiculturalism.

1966
Decimal currency, in the form of dollars and cents, replaces the old pounds, shillings and pence.

1973
Queen Elizabeth II opens the Sydney Opera House.

1975
Dismissal of the Whitlam Labor Government by the Queen's representative, the Governor General.

1988
On 26 January 200 years of European settlement are celebrated.

1996
Massacre at Port Arthur leads to strict gun control legislation.

1999
Australians vote against

Aboriginal 'X-ray' cave painting at Nourlangie Rock in Kakadu National Park

becoming a republic in a national referendum.

2000
Sydney hosts the Olympic Games.

11

Natural Australia

Australia's 'nasties'
Some of Australia's wildlife is not quite as appealing as the much loved koala. Crocodiles inhabit the far north, sharks frequent the continent's seas, and there are many species of venomous snakes. Insect pests include mosquitoes and ants, while certain spiders – particularly the redback and the funnel-web – are to be avoided at all costs. There is no need to panic, however, as visitors are most unlikely to run into any of these 'nasties'.

It is easy to get away from it all in Australia, a vast country which – other than around the coastal fringe – is populated very sparsely. Even the large but relatively uncrowded cities offer many spots where you can find peace and quiet, with plenty of parks and gardens within their precincts. All the major cities are close to either beaches or waterways, and there is a national park on the fringe of virtually every state capital.

National Parks and World Heritage Areas

Because of its superb scenery, vast size and low population density, Australia has well over 3,000 national parks and reserves. Some of these – including Kakadu in the Northern Territory – are remote and wild; some

encompass large expanses of spectacular coastline; while others, such as Sydney's magnificent Ku-ring-gai Chase, preserve unspoiled bushland and wildlife habitats just a short drive from the cities.

Australia also has 11 UNESCO World Heritage listings, the most coveted international conservation status. Sites are included on this list for their outstanding natural or cultural significance, and Uluru-Kata Tjuta (Ayers

The 'laughing' kookaburra, a member of the kingfisher family, is one of Australia's best-known birds

Rock and The Olgas) and the Great Barrier Reef are among Australia's inclusions. Such unique and superbly scenic regions offer some of the continent's best natural environments and these are wonderful places to escape from the world of cities, traffic and overcrowding.

Fauna and Flora

The ancient landmass of Australia, once part of the mega-continent of Gondwana, split away from its neighbors some 50 million years ago. This long isolation has produced some extraordinary flora and fauna – much of it found nowhere else on earth – and these can be seen throughout the continent's reserves and national parks.

Australia's best-known animals are its marsupials – mammals that give birth to tiny young which go on to develop in the mother's pouch. Kangaroos, wallabies, Tasmanian devils, wombats and their closest relatives,

koalas, are all marsupials. The primitive monotremes are even more extraordinary: although mammals, the spiny echidna and the water-dwelling, billed platypus lay eggs. Reptiles include two types of crocodiles and many snakes, and Australia has a profusion of colorful and noisy birds, such as the splendidly hued lorikeet and the famous 'laughing' kookaburra.

The continent has over 15,000 flowering plant species, including 550 varieties of the classic Australian tree, the eucalyptus. This amazing plant takes many forms and can survive in climates and soils as varied as those of the southern snowfields and the central deserts. There is an incredible range of wild flowers, many of which are found nowhere else, while the far north harbors tropical rainforest so ancient and special that it is World Heritage listed.

The golden blooms of one of Western Australia's wild flowers, many of which are unique to the state

Did you know ?

Another highlight of Australia's wilderness areas is the fascinating evidence of the long Aboriginal occupation of the continent – an incredible era of survival in the most extreme conditions, spanning at least 50,000 years. In Kakadu National Park, for example, you can see superb 20,000-year-old rock art sites, while far north Queensland and Central Australia contain many other locations of indigenous cultural and artistic significance.

Australia's Famous

Errol Flynn (1909–59)
Born in Hobart, Tasmania, the legendary movie star Errol Flynn acted in his first Australian film in 1933. After moving to Hollywood in 1935, he became the epitome of the handsome, swashbuckling hero in films like *Captain Blood* and *Robin Hood*. He made over 60 movies, but was equally famous for his three marriages, divorces and involvement in scandal. His 1959 autobiography was appropriately entitled *My Wicked, Wicked Ways*.

Errol Flynn: once the dashing hero of millions of movie-goers

Pat Rafter

A former world number one tennis player, his climb to the top was one of determination and hard work. Pat Rafter's serve-volley game is the epitome of power tennis. Just voted Australia's most recognizable sports personality, he has a huge following as a fair and decent player in a game which has its fair share of bad sports. Off the court, Pat Rafter has established the 'Cherish the Children' foundation through Brisbane Children's Hospital to help needy kids. Born in Mt Isa in 1972 and brought up on the Sunshine Coast, just north of Brisbane, Pat is the third youngest of nine children.

Dame Joan Sutherland

Most of the the nation's talented classical performers are little known outside Australia, but Dame Joan Sutherland is a remarkable exception. This highly acclaimed Sydney-born opera singer made her debut at London's Covent Garden in 1952, and went on to spend 20 years there as a leading soprano. Her performances drew rave reviews in the USA and Europe, and she was given the name 'La Stupenda' by Italian audiences. Ms Sutherland was made a dame in 1979 and gave her glittering farewell performance at the Sydney Opera House in 1990.

Mel Gibson

Renowned for movies such as *The Bounty* (1984), *Hamlet* (1990) and *Maverick* (1994), Mel Gibson's laid back attitude to filmmaking and his approachability ensure his status as one of the mega-stars of Hollywood. Although he was born in New York in 1956, Mel grew up in Australia, where he attended drama school. He first made a name for himself in George Miller's *Mad Max* in 1979. One of his most popular roles has been the unstable Martin Riggs in the *Lethal Weapon* movies, the fourth of which was released in 1998. Mel made his directorial debut with *The Man Without a Face*, where he again stunned audiences with his considerable talent. In 1996 he won an Oscar as Best Director for *Braveheart*, a movie which received four other awards, including Best Picture.

Top Ten

Cairns and District	16
The Gold Coast	17
The Great Barrier Reef	18–19
Great Ocean Road	20
Kakadu National Park	21
The Kimberley	22
Blue Mountains	23
Sydney Harbour and Sydney Opera House	24
Tasmania's World Heritage Area	25
Uluru-Kata Tjuta National Park	26

Above: *Victoria's Twelve Apostles*
Right: *A Barrier Reef fish*

1
Cairns and District, North Queensland

 50B5

 Tourism Tropical North Queensland: Cnr The Esplanade and Ring Road, Cairns. Port Douglas Tourism Information Centre, 23 Macrossan Street, Port Douglas

 Cairns: (07) 4051 3588; Port Douglas/Daintree: (07) 4099 5599 Kuranda: (07) 4093 7593

 Daily

⊠ To Cairns

♿ Few

✋ Cheap to expensive

❓ Huge variety of accommodation from backpacker to five star. Car rental is relatively expensive but there are many bus services and tours to all popular destinations

For much of the year, tropical Cairns has the perfect climate for boating enthusiasts

Cairns is the perfect base for a superb nature-based holiday allowing trips to the World Heritage listed reefs and rainforests as well as the dry outback.

With its international airport, well-developed tourism infrastructure and proximity to natural attractions such as the Great Barrier Reef, tropical rainforests and Atherton Tableland, Cairns is the 'tourist capital' of North Queensland. Here are dozens of hotels, restaurants and shops, and many options for cruises – as well as diving, fishing or snorkeling trips – to the reef. Excellent beaches stretch to the north and south, and adventure activities like whitewater rafting and bungee jumping are popular. Around town you can visit the Cairns Museum and the Pier Marketplace, or just wander the streets and waterfront to soak up the city's relaxed, tropical atmosphere. North of the city is the pretty coastal town of Port Douglas, while further afield are Mossman and the Daintree rainforests.

Inland from Cairns (100km), the cool upland region of the Atherton Tableland, with its fertile farming land, volcanic lakes, waterfalls and rainforest, presents a striking contrast to the hot, humid coast. Kuranda offers colorful markets, the Butterfly Sanctuary, and a walk-through bird aviary. You can reach Kuranda by road, on the spectacular Skyrail rainforest cableway, or by traveling on the famous Kuranda Scenic Railway, which winds its way up the Great Dividing Range.

For a complete change, take a trip inland to the Gulf Savannah country and sample the hospitality of the Outback locals. Discover the grasslands, wetlands, escarpments and saltpans and check out the Undara Lava Tubes.

2
The Gold Coast, Queensland

Although not to everyone's liking, the brash and sometimes crass Gold Coast reveals a very different side of Australia from its natural wonders.

It would be difficult not to have a good time on this lively, highly developed 70-km strip of coastline to the south of Brisbane. Stretching down to Coolangatta on the New South Wales border, the Gold Coast offers consistently warm temperatures and an average of 300 days of sunshine each year, sandy beaches, and clear blue waters that are perfect for swimming, surfing and all kinds of watersports – as well as a smorgasbord of man-made attractions and entertainment.

The heart of the action is the appropriately named Surfers Paradise, the main town, which offers excellent shopping and dining and a host of nightlife options, including the glossy Jupiters Casino at nearby Broadbeach. Many of the Gold Coast's attractions are particularly appealing to children, and theme parks like Dreamworld, Warner Bros Movie World, Wet 'n' Wild Water World and the excellent Sea World are extremely popular. There are many fine golf courses in the area, you can take a cruise to tranquil South Stradbroke Island, go water-skiing, or even sample the daredevil sport of bungee jumping. The Coast's list of things to do is almost endless.

If you prefer to stay somewhere quieter, however, the southern area around Coolangatta offers a less frenetic pace – and fewer high-rise buildings. This is also the location for Currumbin Wildlife Sanctuary, where you can meet some of Australia's unique wildlife. When you've had enough of the coast, a short trip to the hinterland, particularly to the delightful mountain town of Mt Tamborine, is a rewarding experience. Excellent scenery and a cooler environment, with rainforest walking tracks and a diversity of art and craft shops, make this town a great day trip.

51D1

Coach transfers (from Brisbane)

Gold Coast (from Brisbane)

Brisbane (➤ 48–9)
Byron Bay (➤ 37)

Gold Coast Information Centre: Cavill Avenue, Surfers Paradise
(☎ (07) 5538 4419)
Mon–Fri 8–5, Sat 9–5, Sun 9–3:30

Along with its high-rises and tourist development, the Gold Coast offers wonderful beaches and excellent surf

17

3
The Great Barrier Reef, Queensland

51C4

Proserpine, Townsville, Cairns

To Proserpine, Townsville, Cairns

Queensland Government Travel Centre: Adelaide/ Edward Streets, Brisbane (☎ (07) 3874 2800 or 13 1801 (local callers only); fax (07) 3221 5320) Mon–Fri 8:30–5:30, Sat 9:30–12:30

The Great Barrier Reef is often described as the eighth wonder of the world, and a visit to this marine wonderland will be long remembered.

Running parallel to the Queensland coast for over 2,000km – from Papua New Guinea to just south of the Tropic of Capricorn – the Great Barrier Reef is the world's largest living structure. This extraordinary ecosystem is, in fact, made up of over 2,000 linked reefs and around 700 islands and fringing reefs, and is composed of and built by countless tiny coral polyps and algae. This famous natural attraction is protected by its Great Barrier Reef Marine Park status and World Heritage listing.

The reef itself is home to many different types of coral: some are brightly colored, while others, like the aptly-named staghorns, take on strange formations. The reef's tropical waters host an incredible variety of marine life – everything from tiny, luminously colored fish to sharks, manta rays, turtles and dolphins. There are many ways to

view and explore this fabulous underwater world: scenic flights, boat trips, snorkeling or scuba diving, and glass-bottom or semi-submersible boat trips.

For the very best Great Barrier Reef experience, it is possible to stay right on the reef. The idyllic coral cays of Green Island, Heron Island and Lady Elliot Island offer resort accommodation, while Lady Musgrave is for campers only. Other options are to base yourself at a coastal resort (Townsville, Cairns and Port Douglas in the north, or the Whitsunday Islands further south are the best bets) or on one of the many non-reef islands. Some island suggestions are Lizard, Dunk and Magnetic Island in the north; Hayman, South Molle and Hamilton in the Whitsunday region; and Great Keppel Island in the south.

The wonders of the Great Barrier Reef:
Above: *A close underwater encounter*
Left: *Green Island, a true coral cay*

4
Great Ocean Road, Victoria

A journey along Australia's most spectacular road reveals superb coastal scenery, charming old resorts and fishing villages, and a forested hinterland.

60B1

None: driving is recommended

West Coast Railway to Warrnambool only

Ballarat (➤ 63)

Geelong and the Great Ocean Road Visitor Information Centre, Princes Highway, Geelong (☎ 1800 620 888 (toll free) or (03) 5275 5797) Daily 9–5. Closed 25 Dec

Extending from Torquay to Port Fairy, Victoria's Great Ocean Road snakes its way along the state's south-west coast for a distance of 300km. Geelong, 75km from Melbourne, is a good starting point and nearby Bells Beach, one of Australia's surfing meccas, is a good spot to get in the mood for this oceanside drive.

The quiet holiday village of Anglesea is famous for the kangaroos which roam the local golf course, while Lorne offers fine beaches, a delightful seaside resort atmosphere, and forested hillsides inland. Beyond here lies the fishing town of Apollo Bay and magnificent Otway National Park – an irresistible combination of rugged coastline and lush inland rainforest.

The coast becomes more dramatic as you reach Port Campbell National Park. This much photographed coastline is the result of erosion caused by wind, rain and the stormy Southern Ocean – a process which has created spectacular formations. The picturesque town of Port Campbell, with its port, historical museum and self-guided heritage trail, is the ideal base for exploring this very special area.

Further west along this wild coastline, the aptly named Shipwreck Coast is famous for the migrating whales which give birth here between May and August each year, while the town of Warrnambool offers the interesting Flagstaff Hill Maritime Museum, a re-created 19th-century village. The Great Ocean Road proper ends at the charming fishing village of Port Fairy, where there are over 50 National Trust listed buildings, beaches and coastal cruises to enjoy.

Port Campbell National Park encompasses some of Australia's most dramatic coastal scenery

5

Kakadu National Park, Northern Territory

Australia's largest national park is both a superb tropical wilderness and a treasure house of ancient Aboriginal art and culture.

Contrasts of Kakadu – blue sky, rugged cliffs, and a waterhole

Covering almost 20,000sq km to the east of Darwin, this vast World Heritage registered national park is one of Australia's most spectacular attractions. Much of Kakadu is a flat, river-crossed floodplain that is transformed into a lake during the wet season, but this large area is backed by forested lowlands, hills, and the dramatic 250-m cliffs of the Arnhem Land escarpment. The extraordinary wildlife within this varied terrain ranges from dangerous estuarine crocodiles to dingoes, wallabies, snakes, goannas and 275 species of bird.

There is much evidence of the area's long Aboriginal occupation, which may have endured for an incredible 50,000 years. Aboriginal-owned Kakadu includes Nourlangie and Obirr rocks, where you can see fine examples of Aboriginal painting, estimated to be around 20,000 years old. Among the park's scenic highlights are the spectacular Jim Jim Falls and Twin Falls that tumble off the escarpment, and Yellow Water – a tranquil waterhole and wetlands area, home to prolific birdlife.

During the Top End's wet season (November to April) many of the roads are impassable, so the best time to visit Kakadu is during the 'dry'– from May to October. Much of the park can be explored in a normal vehicle, but a four-wheel drive is necessary for off-road traveling. General information is available from the main Visitor Centre, but the Warradjan Aboriginal Cultural Centre at Yellow Water provides a deeper insight into the area's indigenous culture and history. To see something of modern Aboriginal life, you can visit neighboring Arnhem Land; this is Aboriginal land and permits are required to visit, so a tour is the only real option.

✚ 78B5

🍴 Cafés in the area ($–$$)

✖ To Jabiru

♿ Few

✋ Moderate

ℹ Bowali Visitor Centre, Kakadu Highway (☎ (08) 8938 1100) 🕐 Visitor Centre: daily 8–5

❓ Guided walks and tours from the Visitor Centre.

6
The Kimberley, Western Australia

In the far north of Western Australia, the Kimberley is one of the continent's remotest and most spectacular regions.

Explored and settled as late as the 1880s, the Kimberley is extremely rugged and very sparsely settled – the population of less than 30,000 lives in Aboriginal settlements, on enormous cattle stations, and in a few small towns. This vast region of 350,000sq km is generally divided into two main areas, the West and East Kimberley.

The tropical town of Broome, with its multicultural population, pearling history and fabulous beaches, is the ideal starting point for exploring the western region. The nearby settlement of Derby has an interesting Royal Flying Doctor Service base, while inland attractions include the dramatic Geikie Gorge National Park, with its 14km-long gorge.

You can reach the East Kimberley by driving north and east from Broome or flying to Kununurra, a town near the Northern Territory border and the base for the ambitious 1960s and 1970s Ord River Irrigation Scheme. This project

An early sunset over the East Kimberley highlights the rock formations and casts dramatic shadows

created the vast Argyle and Kununurra lakes – welcome breaks in the otherwise arid landscape. From here you can visit the Argyle Diamond Mine, then travel north to the remote port of Wyndham, or south to the wondrous Bungle Bungles. Contained within Purnululu National Park and 'discovered' only in 1983, these spectacular rock formations, up to 300m high, are composed of extremely friable striped silica and sandstone eroded into beehive-like shapes.

Other attractions worth seeing in this wild, last-frontier landscape include the Aboriginal rock art sites of Mirima National Park near Kununurra; Windjana Gorge National Park, reached via the small town of Fitzroy Crossing; and the amazing Wolfe Creek Crater – an enormous depression created by a meteorite falling to earth.

28B4

To Broome or Kununurra

West Tourist Bureau: Bagot Street/Great Northern Highway, Broome. East Tourist Bureau, Coolibah Drive, Kununurra
Broome Tourist Bureau: (☎ (08) 9192 2222; fax (08) 9192 2063).
Kununurra Tourist Bureau: (☎ (08) 9168 1177; fax (08) 9168 2598) ⓞ Daily, generally 9–4

Best visited Apr–Oct, and rental of a four-wheel drive vehicle is recommended. Purnululu National Park closed Jan–Mar

7

Blue Mountains, New South Wales

For a complete change to Sydney's glamour, visit these nearby mountains to experience the great natural beauty of their geological wonders.

✠ 39D3

🚌 From Sydney to most locations; driving is another option

ℹ️ Visitor Information Centre, Great Western Highway, Glenbrook: Visitor Centre
☎ 1300 653 408
🕐 Daily 9–5

♿ Few

❓ A wide range of accommodation from B&Bs to five star. Many tour companies operate day tours from Sydney

These are one of Australia's most popular holiday destinations. Visitors come to the Blue Mountains to experience their wild grandeur, mist-filled valleys, rich Aboriginal and European heritage, and to escape the summer heat. The cold winters allow visitors to enjoy the charm of open fires. Just two hours by road from Sydney, the mountains get their name from their blue haze.

There is so much to do and see here, from just taking in the panoramic views from the many escarpment lookouts to walking in the temperate rainforests which line the ravines and valleys. Waterfalls cascade off the cliffs into valleys far below, where they join streams that disappear into dense vegetation. The golden brown of ancient, weathered rockfaces, formed by the action of the elements over millions of years, contrasts with the distinctive blue green of the mountain vegetation.

Because of the great range and diversity of land forms and plant communities, and its habitats sheltering rare or endangered fauna, the Blue Mountains National Park is being proposed as a World Heritage Area. In addition to its natural sights, there are myriad galleries, antique shops, exquisite gardens, museums and fine eating establishments to enjoy. The Katoomba Scenic Railway and the Scenic Skyway provide unique perspectives of their surroundings while just over the range are the famous Jenolan Caves with their amazing limestone formations.

The entire Blue Mountains region is heavily timbered with eucalypts which constantly disperse droplets of oil into the air, causing the blue light-rays from the sun to be scattered more effectively, which makes distant objects appear blue

23

8
Sydney Harbour &
Sydney Opera House

✚ 33C5

✉ Sydney Opera House: Bennelong Point, Sydney

☎ Sydney Opera House: (02) 9250 7111 for tours, (02) 9250 7209 for details of performances

🕐 Sydney Opera House: guided one-hour tours 9–4 on most days

🍴 Bennelong restaurant ($$$), cafés ($)

🚋 Circular Quay

♿ Good

✋ Moderate

↔ Mrs Macquaries Point, the Domain and Royal Botanic Gardens (▶ 36)

❓ Markets and free musical entertainment on Sun

A classic Australian scene – Sydney's beautiful harbor, graced by its world-famous Opera House and Harbour Bridge

Complemented by the ethereal, sail-like outlines of the famous Opera House, Sydney Harbour is the glittering jewel of Australia's most exciting city.

From the day in January 1788 when the 11 convict-bearing ships of the First Fleet sailed into Port Jackson, Sydney's harbor has been the focus of this great city. A harbor cruise – be it on a luxury boat or a humble Sydney ferry – is a must. From the water you will see the city, including the large areas of bushland of the Sydney Harbour National Park, from a new perspective. Ferries are also the best way to reach waterfront suburbs and the harbor's delightful beaches. From Circular Quay you can take a trip to the beaches of Manly on the north side of the harbor, or to the charming southside suburb of Watsons Bay, close to the harbor's entrance. Ferries also visit some of the national park's islands, including historic Fort Denison.

On the harbor's southern shore, the curved roofs of the Sydney Opera House soar above Bennelong Point. Completed in 1973, after 14 years and many technical and political problems, this architectural masterpiece, designed by Dane Joern Utzon, still inspires controversy. There is no doubt, however, that the structure's stone platform and dramatic white roofs, covered with over a million ceramic tiles, have made it one of the world's most distinctive and unusual buildings. Once you have inspected the exterior, attending a performance or taking a guided tour of the five performance halls is highly recommended. Looming above the magnificent harbor is the third ingredient of this classic Sydney scene – the grand old Sydney Harbour Bridge, completed in 1932 and, with a tunnel opened in 1992, still the major link between the south and north shores (▶ 35).

9
Tasmania's World Heritage Area

Much of the island of Tasmania is superb wilderness, and the state's relatively small size means these untouched areas are easily accessible.

Tasmania's wilderness is of such significant natural beauty that around 20 per cent – an incredible 1.38 million hectares – of the state is under World Heritage protection. This land of rugged peaks, wild rivers, moorland and remote coastline also contains many sites of Aboriginal significance, while the wildlife includes Tasmanian devils, echidnas and the elusive platypus.

One of the most accessible World Heritage regions is the Cradle Mountain-Lake St Clair National Park, just 170km from the capital, Hobart. The alpine scenery here is truly spectacular – high peaks that include Mount Ossa (1,617m), the state's highest mountain, lakes, alpine moorlands and rainforests. There are many hiking tracks here, the most famous of which is the five to ten day Overland Track in the heart of the Cradle Mountain-Lake St Clair National Park.

To the south, the Franklin-Gordon Wild Rivers National Park is particularly famous for its adventurous Franklin River whitewater rafting. Even more remote and untamed wilderness is found in the Southwest National Park, the domain of forests, lakes and a long, deeply indented coastline. Experienced hikers will enjoy the challenge of this park's 85-km South Coast Track. Much closer to Hobart and characterized by its heathlands and rugged dolerite ranges, is the Hartz Mountains National Park.

November to April are the best months to go, but the weather can be unpredictable at any time, changing in minutes from warm and sunny to rain, or even snow.

64B3

From Hobart and/or Launceston to some locations; driving is the best option

To Southwest National Park

Few

Park fees: cheap

Hobart, Launceston, Strahan (► 64–7)

Tasmanian Parks and Wildlife Service: 134 Macquarie Street, Hobart (☎ (03) 6233 6191) Mon–Fri 9–5

A winter scene in Tasmania – Cradle Mountain and Dove Lake, a small part of the state's World Heritage area

10
Uluru-Kata Tjuta National Park, Northern Territory

✝ 78A1

🍴 Cafés and restaurants in the area ($–$$)

✖ Ayers Rock Resort

♿ Few

✋ Park entry fee: moderate

↔ Watarrka National Park (► 80)

ℹ Ayers Rock Visitors Centre: Ayers Rock Resort (☎ (08) 8957 7377 or (08) 8956 2240) ⏰ Daily 8–9

❓ A wide variety of tours is available from the resort: (☎ (08) 8956 2240 for details)

Rising dramatically from the surrounding plains, 348m-high Uluru is an awe-inspiring sight

This 1,325sq km World Heritage–listed park incorporates two of Australia's most spectacular sights – Uluru, better known as Ayers Rock, and neighboring Kata Tjuta (The Olgas).

Located at the center of the continent, Uluru's vast bulk is an extraordinary and overwhelming sight. At 348m high and with a base circumference of some 9km, this is one of the world's largest monoliths – a massive rock which is made even more dramatic by its setting on the monotonous plains of the Red Centre. Uluru was first sighted by Europeans in 1872, but this area has been sacred to Aboriginal people for tens of thousands of years. It is possible to climb the rock, but this can be dangerous and the activity is discouraged by Uluru's Aboriginal owners. Other options are to take a hiking tour of the base, and to view the monolith at sunset, when its normally dark red color changes dramatically as the light fades.

Although, like Uluru, it is the tip of a vast underground formation, Kata Tjuta, 50km to the west, offers a rather different experience. The name means 'many heads' – an appropriate description of the 30 or so massive rocks which make up The Olgas. There are several trails among the formation's gorges and valleys, although most should be undertaken only if you are well prepared.

A visit to the Uluru-Kata Tjuta Cultural Centre, just a kilometer from Uluru, is a must. This excellent complex includes displays on Aboriginal culture and history, demonstrations of traditional art and dance, and a shop that sells local arts and crafts. The base for exploring the national park is the well-designed Ayers Rock Resort

What To See

New South Wales	30-43
Food and Drink	44-5
Queensland	47-55
Victoria and Tasmania	57-67
In the Know	68-9
South Australia and Northern Territory	71-81
Western Australia	83-90

STOP 9

THE SYDNEY EXPLORER

Above: *Camping in the Outback*
Right: *Sydney Explorer bus stop*

27

AUSTRALIA

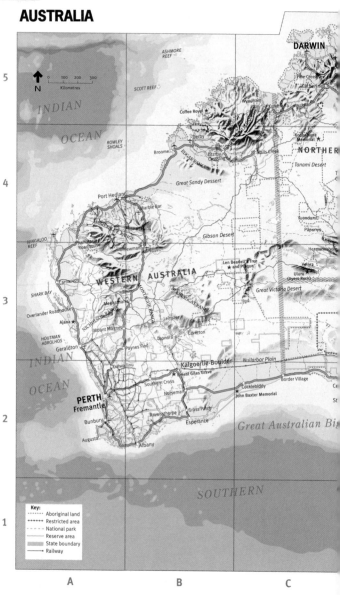

Key:
- ········· Aboriginal land
- ✶✶✶✶✶ Restricted area
- ------- National park
- Reserve area
- State boundary
- —— Railway

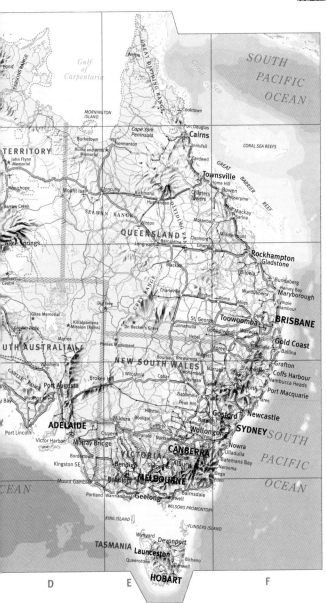

SOUTH
PACIFIC
OCEAN

Gulf of Carpentaria

Weipa

GREAT DIVIDING RANGE

Coral Sea

PARSONS RANGE

...land

Cooktown

MORNINGTON
ISLAND

Cape York
Peninsula

Port Douglas

Cairns

TERRITORY

John Flynn
Memorial

Burketown

Normanton

Innisfail

Cardwell

CORAL SEA REEFS

Wauchope

Mount Isa

Cloncurry

Richmond

Hughenden

Burke and Wills
Memorial

Barrow Creek

SELWYN RANGE

Townsville

Home Hill

Bowen

Proserpine

GREAT

BARRIER

REEF

Charters
Towers

Mackay
Sarina

Alice Springs

Winton

QUEENSLAND

DIVIDING RANGE

Barcaldine

Longreach

Moranbah

Clermont

Middlemount

Emerald

Rockhampton
Gladstone

...ert
Centre

Blackall

Biloela

Giles Memorial

Killalpaninna
Mission (Ruins)

Dig Tree

GREAT
DIVIDING
RANGE

Charleville

Mitchell

Roma

Miles

Mundubbera

Bundaberg

Hervey Bay
Maryborough

Gympie
Nambour

Coober Pedy

Dr. Becker's Grave

Cunnamulla

St. George

Toowoomba

Goondiwindi

Warwick

BRISBANE

Marree

Pooles Monument

Hebel

Gold Coast

...field

Ballina

UTH AUSTRALIA

Woomera

Bourke

Brewarrina

Walgett

Moree

Grafton

Coffs Harbour

Nambucca Heads

GAWLER RANGE

Port Augusta

Broken Hill

Wilcannia

Cobar

NEW SOUTH WALES

Coonamble

Narrabri

...idale

Port Macquarie

...Bay

Whyalla

Nyngan

Peak Hill

Natromine

Taree

Port Lincoln

ADELAIDE

Mildura

Booligal

Hillston

Barh...

Gosford

Newcastle

Victor Harbor

Murray Bridge

Ouyen

Balranald

Griffith

Narrandera

SYDNEY

SOUTH

Kingston SE

Bordertown

VICTORIA

CANBERRA

Shepparton

Albury

Wollongong

Nowra

Ulladulla

PACIFIC

Mount Gambier

Bendigo

...

Batemans Bay

Naroona

Bega

Ballarat

MELBOURNE

Eden

OCEAN

Portland

Warrnambool

Geelong

Colwell

Bairnsdale

WILSONS PROMONTORY

...CEAN

KING ISLAND

Wynyard

Devonport

FLINDERS ISLAND

TASMANIA

Launceston

Bicheno

Queenstown

...well

HOBART

D

E

F

New South Wales

New South Wales, named by Cook in 1770 because it reminded him of south Wales, is Australia's fourth largest state but has the largest population – almost 6.2 million. Geographically, it forms a series of parallel strips: a narrow coastal plain which supports the bulk of the population, the uplands of the Great Dividing Range, slopes and plains which form the state's agricultural heartland and, finally, the Outback. The climate varies from subtropical in the north to the winter snows of the mountains in the far south. Although within the boundaries of New South Wales, the Australian Capital Territory is governed and administered separately. The territory and the national capital, Canberra, were created early this century to resolve the long-running rivalry between Sydney and Melbourne over which city should be the nation's capital.

' … few cities on earth have arrived at so agreeable a fulfilment … they are very lucky people, whose fates have washed them up upon this brave and generally decent shore. '

JAN MORRIS ON SYDNEY
Among the Cities (1983)

Sydney

The nation's birthplace has developed from its humble convict beginnings into a vibrant metropolis that holds its own on the world stage. With a multicultural population of over 3.8 million, Sydney is the continent's largest and, many would say, most brash city. Although the pace of life is faster here than anywhere else in Australia, Sydneysiders still know how to relax – the city's harbor, long golden beaches and surrounding bushland make sure of that.

In recent years Sydney has truly come of age as a major city and an enviable tourist destination. It has been voted 'the world's best city' by discerning travelers the world over, but perhaps the biggest accolade of all came when Sydney was chosen as the host city for the 2000 Summer Olympic Games. There is plenty to see and do: in addition to the fascinating convict history, museums, galleries and, of course, the 'Great Outdoors', the city offers wonderful shopping, an innovative and highly acclaimed restaurant scene and a wide choice of nightlife.

Although visitors spend most of their time in the inner city and eastern suburbs, an entirely different world lies beyond. To the north lie the glorious Northern Beaches with surf, sand and a far more relaxed lifestyle, the charming waterway of Pittwater, and the bushland of Ku-ring-gai Chase National Park. To the west, you can visit historic Parramatta and Homebush Bay, the Olympic Games site. Sydney's inner suburbs also have a great deal to offer. A visit to famous Bondi, Manly or one of the many other beaches is a must.

Sydney has it all – a modern, upbeat city center, harbor and waterfront and a relaxing way of life

James Cook's 1770 landing at Botany Bay, south of Sydney, is marked by a modest monument

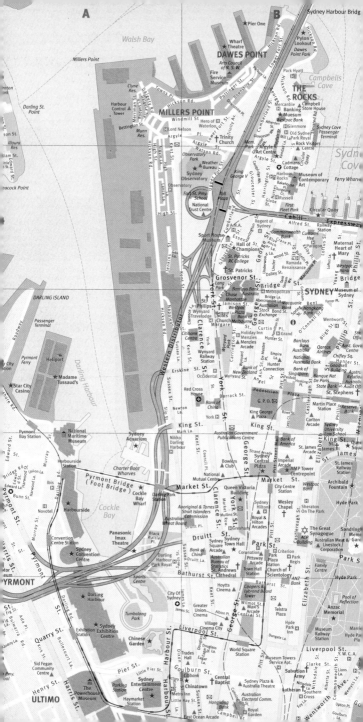

CENTRAL SYDNEY

Port Jackson

FORT DENISON

N

0   0.1   0.2   0.3
Kilometres

Bennelong Point

Sydney Opera House
Opera House
Man O'War Jetty

Mrs. Macquaries Point

Government House

Mrs. Macquarie's Chair

ADI Garden Island Naval Dockyard Facility

GARDEN ISLAND

Farm Cove

The Domain

The Andrew (Boy) Charlton Pool

ADI Naval Dockyard

Conservatorium of Music

Royal Botanic Gardens

Woolloomooloo Bay

Captain Cook Graving Dock

Dock Basin

Boat Harbour

Restaurant & Kiosk

Sydney Tropical Centre

Visitor Centre

National Herbarium

Cahill Expressway

State Library of New South Wales

The Domain

Art Gallery Rd.

Art Gallery of N.S.W.

The Domain

Cowper Wharf Roadway

Wylde St.

Grantham Lodge

Oak La.
St. Neot Av.

Grantham St.

Florida Motor Inn

McDonald St.

McDonald La.

Elizabeth Ba

ELIZABETH BAY

Challis Av.

St Vincents School & Crt.

Chateau Sydney

Olims Sydney

Athur McElhone Res.

Wharf

Lincoln Cr.

Cowper Wharf Roadway

Bland St.

Nicholson St.

Rockwall Cr.

Rockwall La.

Dorchester

POTTS POINT

Victoria St.

Nesbitt St.

Harnett St.

Bourke St.

Wilson St.

Hordens St.

Rowena Pl.

Devere

Manhattan

Crick Av.

Elizabeth Bay House

Greenknowe Av.

Elizabeth

Plunkett St.

Griffiths St.

McElhone St.

Broughton St.

Tusculum St.

The Macquarie Private

Macleay St.

Rex

Roslyn Gardens Motor Inn

Parking Station

Harmer St.

Plunkett St. Pmy. School

St. Columbkille

Forbes St.

Stephen St.

Hughes St.

Merlin St.

Orwell St.

Springfield Av.

Spring

Kellett St.

Bernly Private

Gazebo Ramada

Sebel Town House

Tennis Courts

Sydney Eye Hospital

Bossley Tce.

Sydney

Victoria Towers

Rae St.

Park Lane Arcade

Elizabeth Bay Rd.

Police

Cathedral St.

Junction La.

Junction St.

Earl Crt. Serv. Aparts.

Earl Pl.

Macleay St.

Motel Lodge

WOOLLOOMOOLOO

Cathedral

Reid St.

Brougham St.

Ward Av.

St. Lukes Hospital

Tennis Courts

Sylvia Chase Sq.

Judge St.

KINGS CROSS

Ilett St.

Roslyn St.

St. Comices RC Sch.

Crown St.

Broughton La.

Dowling St.

Darlinghurst Rd.

Elizabeth

Kennedy St.

Robinson St.

McCarthy St.

Sutter St.

Earl Crt.

Kings Cross Station

Roslyn Pl.

Ashdown

Australian Tourist Commission

Sydney Boulevarde

McElhone St.

Brougham St.

Mansion La.

Plainsman Motor Inn

Clement La.

Rushcu

EAST SYDNEY

William St.

Yurong La.

Barnett La.

William St.

Premier

Kings Cross Station Brougham

Hampton St.

Mansions

Bayswater Park

Plaza Suites

Clement Av.

Travelo

School of Visual Art

St. Peters La.

St. Peters

Cobb Bayswater

Goderich St.

Surrington

Hard Rock Cafe

Stanley St.

Chapel St.

O'Briens La.

Sydney Church of England Grammar School for Girls

Roslyn La.

Farrell Av.

Kingsgate

King Cross Road

Francis St.

Hargrave La.

Crown St.

Stanley La.

Liberal Catholic

First Church of Christ Scientist Catholic

Bourke St.

Forbes St.

Tewkesbury

Kirketon

St Johns

Craigend St.

Liverpool St.

Berwick La.

Shorter La.

Mont Clair

Darley Pl.

Whites La.

Hayden La.

Camelot La.

Surrey La.

Surrey St.

Womerah

Barcom Av.

Nield Av.

Burton St.

Bourke St.

St. Vincents Caritas Centre

Sydney Jewish Museum

Burton St.

DARLINGHURST

Darlinghurst Pmy. School

Liverpool St.

Boundary St.

Gosbell St.

Neild Av.

McLachlan Av.

Oxford St.

Koala

Kells La.

Foley St.

What to See in Sydney

AMP TOWER   ✪✪✪

The best view in town is from the top of the 304.8-m AMP Tower. From the observation level there are superb 360-degree views of the city and its surrounds. The tower has two revolving restaurants, particularly spectacular at night.

AUSTRALIAN MUSEUM   ✪✪✪

A world-class natural history museum, this is an excellent place to learn about pre-European Aboriginal life and Australia's native fauna. Also featured are human evolution, minerals, dinosaurs and Pacific and Indonesian cultures.

DARLING HARBOUR   ✪✪✪

With its harborside shopping and eating complex, the delightful Chinese Garden, the Imax Theatre and National Maritime Museum, Darling Harbour is one of Sydney's most popular recreation areas. One of the best attractions is the **Sydney Aquarium**, where you will encounter sharks, crocodiles and colorful Great Barrier Reef fish at close quarters. The futuristic building of the National Maritime Museum contains six galleries covering maritime themes as diverse as the discovery of Australia and surfboard technology. Moored outside are various vessels, including a World War II destroyer and a Russian submarine. Many of the exhibits are interactive in this stimulating museum.

Sidebar (left column):

✚ 32B2
✉ Centrepoint
☎ (02) 9229 7444
🕐 Sun–Fri 9:30–9:30, Sat 9:30AM–11:30PM

✚ 33C2
✉ 6 College Street
☎ (02) 9320 6000
🕐 Daily 9:30–5. Closed 25 Dec

✚ 32A3
✉ Darling Harbour
☎ 1902 260 568
🕐 Daily 9:30–5. Closed 25 Dec
♿ Excellent
🍴 Moderate
🍴 Café ($–$$)

Sydney Aquarium
☎ (02) 9262 2300
🕐 Daily 9:30–10
🚝 Monorail to Darling Park
♿ Very good
🍴 Expensive

Right: Darling Harbour's beautifully designed Chinese Garden provides a tranquil oasis in the heart of the city

Facing page: *An unusual view of the Sydney Harbour Bridge from the harbor's north shore*

POWERHOUSE MUSEUM ⭐⭐

Sydney's largest museum is an entertaining technological and cultural wonderland with everything from a huge 18th-century steam engine and a 1930s art deco cinema to holograms and irresistible hands-on computer displays.

+ 32A1
✉ 500 Harris Street, Ultimo
☎ (02) 9217 0111
🕐 Daily 10–5. Closed 25 Dec

THE ROCKS ⭐⭐⭐

With its intriguing past and prime harborside location, this is Sydney's tourist mecca. The Rocks was the site of Australia's first 'village', and the region has had a colorful history. In addition to wandering the narrow streets, sitting on the waterfront and browsing in the many shops, Rocks highlights are a lively weekend market and several small museums – including the Sydney Observatory at nearby Millers Point. Full details of the area are available from the Information Centre.

+ 32B5
✉ Visitor Information Centre, 106 George Street
☎ 13 2077
🕐 Daily 9–5
🚊 Circular Quay
🎫 Free

SYDNEY HARBOUR (▶ 24, TOP TEN)

SYDNEY HARBOUR BRIDGE ⭐⭐

Completed in 1932, this famous bridge is still the primary link between the harbor's north and south shores, although the Sydney Harbour Tunnel now handles a large share of the traffic. You can inspect the bridge from close up by taking the walkway from the Rocks, and then climbing the 200 steps of the Pylon. For really spectacular views of the harbor and city, take the BridgeClimb tour.

+ 32B5
✉ Pylon Lookout
☎ (02) 9247 3408 BridgeClimb: (02) 9252 0077
🕐 Daily 10–5. Closed 25 Dec
🚊 Circular Quay, then a walk
♿ None
🎫 Cheap

SYDNEY OPERA HOUSE (▶ 24, TOP TEN)

TARONGA ZOO ⭐⭐

Reached by a scenic ferry ride, Taronga is visited as much for its harborside location as for the opportunity to meet native Australian wildlife. All the well-known marsupials and monotremes – including koalas, kangaroos, echidnas, wombats and Tasmanian devils – are here, as well as indigenous birds and reptiles, and a large collection of exotic creatures like Sumatran tigers and elephants.

+ Off map
✉ Bradleys Head Road, Mosman
☎ 0055 20218
🕐 Daily 9–5
🍴 Cafés ($$) and kiosk ($)
🚢 Taronga Zoo wharf
♿ Good 🎫 Charge

35

Opera House, Royal Botanic Gardens & Macquarie Street

Distance
3km

Time
2–4 hours, depending on
Opera House and museum
visits

Start point
Circular Quay
✚ 32B4
Ⓠ Circular Quay

End point
Circular Quay
✚ 32B4
Ⓠ Circular Quay

Lunch
Botanic Gardens Restaurant
and Kiosk ($$)
✉ Royal Botanic Gardens
☎ (02) 9241 2419

This enjoyable walk combines a harbor foreshore stroll with visits to an art gallery and some historic buildings.

Start at Circular Quay.

Lively Circular Quay is the focus of the city's ferry system. There are many cafés in the area, which is famous for its offbeat entertainers.

Follow the Circular Quay East walkway towards the Opera House.

Inspect the exterior of Australia's most famous building, then take a guided tour of the performance halls.

Enter the Botanic Gardens via the gate near the Opera House.

Sydney's waterfront **Royal Botanic Gardens** contain an outstanding collection of native and imported flora. The lush Sydney Tropical Centre is one of the highlights here.

After exploring the gardens, continue around the foreshore to the eastern side of the cove.

From the headland known as Mrs Macquaries Point there are classic views of Sydney Harbour, the Opera House and the Harbour Bridge.

Head south along Mrs Macquaries Road until you reach the Art Gallery.

The Art Gallery of New South Wales is the state's premier gallery, with superb examples of Australian, Aboriginal, European and Asian art. By the gallery is The Domain, a large parkland area.

Follow Art Gallery Road until you reach College Street, then turn right.

Gracious Macquarie Street contains many historic buildings, including the 1819 Hyde Park Barracks, once a home for convicts but now a fascinating museum, and The Mint (1816), a museum devoted to gold.

Continue along Macquarie Street, then turn left into Albert Street to return to Circular Quay.

The historic buildings of Sydney's Rocks area (foreground) contrast with the modern high-rises that surround Circular Quay

A sandy stretch of coastline near Coffs Harbour on the north coast

What to See in New South Wales

BLUE MOUNTAINS (► 23, TOP TEN)

BROKEN HILL ✪

A visit to the state's Outback is recommended – this harsh sunbaked land is a completely different world, far removed from Sydney's glossy waterside ambience. The silver-mining town of Broken Hill, in the far west, is a good Outback destination. Here you can tour one of the mines, visit the Royal Flying Doctor Service base, and take a trip to nearby Kinchega National Park, or the mining ghost town of Silverton.

🞦 38A4
🚉 Broken Hill
✈ Air from Sydney
🛈 Broken Hill Tourist Information Centre: Blende/Bromide Streets (☎ (08) 8087 6077) ◷ Daily 8:30–5. Closed 25 Dec

BYRON BAY ✪✪

Paradise for beach lovers, with golden beaches, a wonderful climate, clear blue waters and pounding surf, 'Byron' attracts surfers, scuba divers and holidaymakers in droves. You can walk to Cape Byron (mainland Australia's most easterly point), visit Byron Bay Whale Centre, or just browse around the many art and craft shops. Take a drive to the hinterland rainforests or the hippie town of Nimbin.

🞦 39F5
✈ Ballina or Lismore, then a drive
🛈 Byron Bay Visitor Information Centre: Jonson Street (☎ (02) 6685 8050) ◷ Daily 9–5. Closed Good Fri, 25 Dec

COFFS HARBOUR ✪✪

Tourism and banana growing are the main industries of this north coast city, which offers excellent beaches and a warm, sunny climate. Other attractions include the Big Banana Leisure Park and the Pet Porpoise Pool, while a drive inland to the picturesque upland town of Bellingen and the rainforests of World Heritage-listed Dorrigo National Park is highly recommended.

🞦 39F4
🚉 Coffs Harbour
🛈 Coffs Harbour Visitor Information Centre: Rose Avenue/Marcia Street (☎ (02) 6652 1522) ◷ Daily 9–5. Closed Good Fri, 25 Dec

KIAMA ✪✪

One of the closest South Coast seaside resorts to Sydney, the small town of Kiama has long enjoyed great popularity. As well as good beaches and surfing, the town has a famous blowhole and many historic buildings. Inland, Kiama is close to charmingly rural Kangaroo Valley and the Minnamurra Rainforest Reserve.

🞦 39D2
🚉 Kiama
🛈 Kiama Visitors Information Centre, Blowhole Point Road, Kiama (☎ (02) 4232 3322) ◷ Daily 9–5. Closed 25 Dec

37

✛ 39E3

🚌 Maitland, then a bus to
Cessnock

ℹ Cessnock Visitor
Information Centre:
Turner Park, Aberdare
Road (☎ (02) 4990
4477) ⏰ Weekdays
9–5, Sat 9:30–5, Sun
9:30–3:30. Closed 25 Dec

HUNTER VALLEY ●●●

Wine and wineries are the main attraction of this large river valley northwest of Sydney, centered around the towns of Cessnock and Pokolbin. Grapes have been cultivated here since the 1830s and there are now over 50 wineries in the region; many of these can be toured and you can, of course, sample the fine wines that originate from the area. The Hunter also has a reputation for excellent accommodation and dining, making it a very popular weekend destination for Sydneysiders.

NEW SOUTH WALES

39

<table>
<tr><td>

✚ Off map
✗ Air from Sydney and
  Brisbane
ℹ Lord Howe Island Tourist
  Centre: (☎ (02) 9244
  1777); Island Visitors
  Centre: (☎ (02) 6563
  2114) 🕐 Mon–Fri
  9–12:30

✚ 39E3
☎ (02) 4987 3108
🕐 Daily
♿ Few
💰 Free
❓ No public transport into
  the park

✚ 39C2
Kosciuszko National Park
✉ Snowy Region Visitor
  Centre, Kosciuszko Road,
  Jindabyne
☎ (02) 6450 5600
🕐 Daily 8–6; 7–7 Jan, Easter
  and snow season
🚌 Jindabyne and Thredbo.
  Perisher Blue (ski season)

✚ 39D2
🚉 Mittagong, Bowral or
  Moss Vale
ℹ Information Centre: 62–70
  Main Street, Mittagong
  (☎ (02) 4871 2888)
  🕐 Daily 8–5:30. Closed
  25 Dec

</td></tr>
</table>

LORD HOWE ISLAND ⭐⭐

A true South Sea paradise. Dominated by sheer peaks this World Heritage-listed small island is just 11km long and 2km at its widest. The high peaks and lower, scattered hills were created by volcanic activity, and below these lie Kentia palm forests, idyllic sandy beaches, a fringing coral reef, and the clear blue waters of the island's lagoon, home to over 500 fish species. Visitors are well catered for with various grades of accommodations.

MYALL LAKES NATIONAL PARK ⭐

This North Coast national park encompasses both a chain of large freshwater lakes and an idyllic 40km coastline. You can hire a houseboat or canoe to explore the lakes, or camp and enjoy surfing and swimming off the golden beaches. The area is particularly appealing to birdwatchers and bushwalkers.

SNOWY MOUNTAINS ⭐⭐

In the state's far south, reached via the town of Jindabyne, this upland region encompasses **Kosciuszko National Park**, where you can ski in winter from the resorts of Thredbo and Perisher Blue. The wilderness park contains heathland and alpine vegetation, as well as Mount Kosciuszko, Australia's highest point (just 2,228m). In summer the area is great for bushwalking, trout fishing, horse riding and mountain biking.

SOUTHERN HIGHLANDS ⭐⭐⭐

Just 100km from Sydney, this upland region offers a blend of rugged Australian bush, rolling English-type farmland and genteel townships. Colonial history is well represented: the charming village of Berrima dates from 1831 and is full of historic buildings. You can shop for crafts and antiques in Berrima, Moss Vale and Bowral, and go bushwalking in the Morton National Park.

The Blue Mountains

This drive takes you to one of Sydney's favorite recreation areas – the rugged and scenic Blue Mountains.

From central Sydney, drive west along Parramatta Road, which joins the Western Motorway (Route 4). Continue until you see the signs for the Great Western Highway.

After Glenbrook (information centre), continue to the Norman Lindsay Gallery and Museum at Faulconbridge, devoted to one of Australia's most celebrated artists and writers. Wentworth Falls offers the historic house of Yester Grange and the Falls Reserve.

Continue on the highway until you reach the Leura turnoff.

The picturesque town of Leura has cafés, crafts shops and the cool-climate Everglades Gardens.

Take the signposted scenic Cliff Drive to nearby Katoomba.

This brings you to Echo Point with spectacular views of the Three Sisters, the surrounding cliffs, and the forested Jamison Valley.

Continue on the Cliff Drive, which rejoins the Great Western Highway. Follow the signs to Blackheath.

In Blackheath, head for the National Parks and Wildlife Service Heritage Centre, and a splendid panorama.

Keep following the Great Western Highway to Mount Victoria.

Mount Victoria is classifed as an Urban Conservation Area and has a museum, teashops and a few antique shops.

Follow the Darling Causeway then turn right on to the Bells Line of Road.

Visit Mount Tomah Botanic Garden, a branch of Sydney's Royal Botanic Gardens.

Continue to Windsor, then follow Route 40, and the Western Motorway.

Distance
280km

Time
A full day, or stay overnight if possible

Start point
George Street, central Sydney
32B2

A view of the famous Three Sisters rock formation from Echo Point near Katoomba

End point
George Street, central Sydney
32B2

Lunch
Café Bon Ton ($–$$)
192 The Mall, Leura
(02) 4782 4377

41

Facing page: *Canberra's vast Parliament House, opened in 1988, is topped by an 81m-high flagpole*

Below: *The planned city of Canberra is an attractive environment of parks, lakeland and leafy suburbs*

✉ Clunies Ross Street, Acton
☎ (02) 6250 9540; fax (02) 6250 9599
🕐 Daily 9–5 (to 8PM in Jan). Closed 25 Dec
🍴 Café ($)
♿ Good
🎫 Free

Canberra and the Australian Capital Territory

Created out of New South Wales farmland after its site was designated in 1908, Canberra is a planned city unlike anywhere else in the nation. Designed by American architect Walter Burley Griffin, and surrounded by parks and gardens, the national capital is a pleasant environment. Canberra is the home of Australia's Federal government; half of the 300,000 population is employed in this area. The city is full of diplomatic missions and government departments, and – appealing for the visitor – national museums and galleries. The central focus is man-made Lake Burley Griffin, a location for cruises, from where radial roads lead out to suburbs and wild bushland. Beyond the city center, the surrounding Australian Capital Territory (ACT) offers rugged Namadgi National Park, Tidbinbilla Nature Reserve and 1859 Lanyon Homestead.

What to See in Canberra and the ACT

AUSTRALIAN NATIONAL BOTANIC GARDENS ◆◆

Containing the world's best collection of Australia's unique flora, these gardens feature more than 600 species of eucalyptus trees, a rockery, the delightful rainforest gully, and a Tasmanian alpine garden. Self-guided arrow trails make it easy to find your way around.

Looming behind the gardens is Black Mountain (812m), capped by the futuristic Telstra Tower. There is a spectacular view of the city and surrounding countryside from this structure's viewing gallery.

AUSTRALIAN WAR MEMORIAL ✪✪
In a dramatic location at the head of Anzac Parade, this impressive monument and museum commemorates the Australians who served in various wars. Its many thousands of displays, including aeroplanes, tanks, guns, military memorabilia and artworks, make the War Memorial one of Australia's most visited attractions.

✉ Anzac Parade, Campbell
☎ (02) 6243 4211
🕐 Daily 10–5. Closed 25 Dec
🍴 Café ($)
♿ Very good
🎫 Free

NATIONAL GALLERY OF AUSTRALIA ✪✪✪
This is the nation's premier gallery, and the ideal place to view good examples of Aboriginal and Australian art. European, Asian and American artworks are also featured, and the gallery frequently hosts excellent traveling exhibitions.

✉ Parkes Place, Parkes
☎ (02) 6240 6502
🕐 Daily 10–5. Closed Good Fri, 25 Dec
♿ Very good
🎫 Cheap

PARLIAMENT HOUSE ✪✪✪
Canberra's architectural and political centerpiece was completed in 1988, at a staggering cost of over $1,000 million. It contains the House of Representatives and the Senate, public areas featuring fine artworks and crafts-manship, and hundreds of offices. Guided tours are available, and you can sit in on the often heated debates of afternoon Question Time in the House of Representatives. The view from the roof is superb.

While in this Parliamentary Triangle area, visit the far more modest 1927 Old Parliament House, now housing several interesting exhibitions.

✉ Capital Hill
☎ (02) 6277 5399
🕐 Daily 9–5 (later when Parliament is sitting). Closed 25 Dec
🍴 Café ($–$$)
🚌 231, 901
♿ Excellent
🎫 Free
❓ Advance bookings for Question Time: (☎ (02) 6277 4889)

QUESTACON ✪✪✪
Also known as The National Science and Technology Centre, this exciting, modern complex brings the world of science alive. Education and entertainment are combined brilliantly in the 170 or so interactive exhibits, and intriguing science shows are performed by the center's staff at regular intervals.

✉ King Edward Terrace, Parkes
☎ (02) 6270 2800
🕐 Daily 10–5. Closed 25 Dec
♿ Very good
🎫 Moderate

Food & Drink

It seems almost inconceivable that in the early 1980s Australian food was bland and very much of the traditional English 'meat and two veg' school of cooking: sweet and sour pork or a prawn cocktail were considered the height of culinary sophistication. All this has changed dramatically, largely due to Asian, Middle Eastern and European immigrants introducing their ingredients and styles of cooking.

A World of Food

Australian cuisine is now taking the world by storm – the famous chef Robert Carrier declared on a visit in 1996 that Australian food was the most exciting available, and that it was about to take over the world. Much of this acclaim is due to the development and refinement of 'Modern Australian' cuisine – a form of cooking that has evolved from the use of excellent fresh produce, the fusion of styles and ingredients (anything from Thai to Italian in one dish), and stylish presentation.

An important component of Australia's inventive cuisine is the superb quality and variety of local produce, from tropical fruits like mangoes to Tasmania's wonderful cheeses and the freshest herbs. The quality of meat is very high, and the variety of seafood will astonish many northern hemisphere visitors: enormous prawns, oysters, crabs, lobsters and delicious tropical fish such as barramundi.

A seafood feast at the famous Doyle's on the Beach restaurant in Watsons Bay, Sydney

Australia also offers cuisines from all over the world, with Thai, Japanese and other Asian restaurants being particularly popular. You will find everything from Italian and Greek to Lebanese and African cuisines, and one of the greatest joys in this fine climate is eating alfresco, often with a marvelous water view.

Wine, Beer and Spirits

Wine has been produced in Australia since the late 1830s, and the country's reds and whites are now deservedly world famous. All of the states have some involvement in the industry, but South Australia's Barossa Valley and Coonawarra region, the Hunter Valley of New South Wales, and the Margaret River area of Western Australia are some of the most famous.

Red varieties include Cabernet Sauvignon, Shiraz, Pinot Noir and Merlot, while Chardonnay, Chablis, Sauvignon Blanc and Verdelho are popular whites. There are many hundreds of different labels to choose from, and the best way to discover what you like is to try as many as possible! Ultimately, it all comes down to taste, but it's hard to go wrong with labels like Wolf Blass, Rosemount Estate, Penfolds, Houghtons, and Henschke.

Australian beers are now known throughout the world, and there is a huge range to choose from. In addition to Fosters, Tooheys, VB (Victoria Bitter), Reschs, Cascade, Carlton, Swan and XXXX (Fourex) there are popular regional brands, and aficionados will enjoy specialist beers like Hahn, Coopers, Redback and the curiously named Dogbolter.

A wonderful range of fresh produce forms the basis of modern Australian cuisine

Australia is not renowned for its spirits, although reasonably good brandy is produced in South Australia. Sampling Bundaberg rum – universally known as 'Bundy' and a delicious by-product of the sugar industry in Queensland – is a must. This fine spirit comes as both underproof (37 per cent) and overproof (a lethal 57.7 per cent), and is usually topped up with cola.

A small selection of the fine white wines produced in NSW's Hunter Valley

Queensland

Occupying an enormous chunk of the continent's northeast, Queensland is the second largest state after Western Australia. From the subtropical capital of Brisbane in the far south, this vast tract of land – much of which has a hot, sunny and virtually winterless climate – stretches north to well within the tropics.

Many people come here solely to experience the World Heritage-listed Great Barrier Reef, a magnificent natural wonder which lies parallel to the coast's sandy beaches and idyllic islands. But Queensland offers much more. Behind the coastal strip, and the hills of the Great Dividing Range, stretches the inhospitable Outback, while in the far north are lush tropical rainforests and the rugged and sparsely populated Cape York Peninsula, which ends just south of Papua New Guinea.

' It is often said that Scandinavians find the achievement of plenty linked with mediocrity . . . so dull that many of them either take to drink or commit suicide. Australians are more likely to commit smugness. '

ELSPETH HUXLEY
Their Shining Eldorado (1967)

Brisbane – Australia's third largest city

Brisbane

**From its crude beginnings as a penal colony –
founded in 1824 as an outpost of New South Wales
– and its long-standing reputation as a conservative 'country town', Brisbane has undergone a
remarkable metamorphosis in recent years, and
has embraced progress with much enthusiasm.
With a subtropical climate and relatively small
population of just over a million, the city has a
slower pace of life than that of southern cities, and
Queensland's capital has blossomed into a most
attractive metropolis.**

Although most visitors do not linger for long in Brisbane
before heading south to the Gold Coast or north to the
attractions of the coast and Great Barrier Reef, there is
plenty to see and do here. The city's riverside location is a
very important ingredient of its charm: Brisbane stands on
a sweeping bend of the Brisbane River, and taking a
leisurely cruise or ferry ride around and beyond the city is a
highlight of any visit.

There *are* museums, galleries and a few graceful old
buildings here, but sunny Brisbane is a largely modern city,
concerned for the most part with relaxing and enjoying the
good things in life. The brilliantly designed South Bank
Parklands, which include a swimming lagoon and sandy
beach, and the city's many parks and gardens, are ideal
places to indulge in such pursuits, as are the islands and
beaches of nearby Moreton Bay. You can also explore the
pleasant city center – particularly the shops and outdoor
cafés of Queen Street Mall; the Riverside Centre and its
ferry wharves, just off Eagle Street; and King George
Square. The best view of Brisbane is from the lookout at
the top of nearby Mt Coot-tha.

What to See in Brisbane
CITY BOTANIC GARDENS ✪✪
Brisbane's premier gardens are in a delightful riverside setting and provide the ideal spot for a break from sight-seeing and the heat. The gardens are open around the clock and you can wander among the palm trees, Bunya Pines and rainforest area, or take a guided walk.

- ✉ Alice Street
- ☎ (07) 3403 7911
- 🍴 Café ($–$$)
- 🚌 City Circle 333
- ♿ Very good
- 🎫 Free

MOUNT COOT-THA ✪✪
It's worth making the trip to this peak, 8km from the city center, especially at night, for the wonderful view of Brisbane and its surrounds. There is an excellent restaurant and a café here, and you can visit the **Mount Coot-tha Botanic Gardens**, with their tropical and native flora, hiking tracks and Aboriginal trails, as well as the Cosmic Skydome and Planetarium, where a dramatic image of the night sky is projected onto a dome.

Botanic Gardens
- ✉ Toowong
- ☎ (07) 3403 2550
- 🕐 Daily 8–5.30
- 🍴 Café ($); restaurant ($$)
- 🚌 37A
- ♿ Good
- 🎫 Gardens free, Skydome moderate

QUEENSLAND CULTURAL CENTRE ✪✪✪
This large, modern South Bank complex includes two important museums – the Queensland Art Gallery, with its fine collection of Australian, Aboriginal, Asian, Pacific and European art; and the Queensland Museum with some particularly good Aboriginal and natural history displays. The nearby State Library has an excellent bookshop.

- ➕ ☎ Art Gallery: (07) 3840 7303. Museum: 7555
- 🕐 Daily: Art Gallery 10–5, Museum 9–5. Closed Good Fri, 25 Dec
- ♿ Good
- 🎫 Free

SOUTH BANK PARKLANDS ✪✪✪
This large riverside area, south of the city center and the site of the 1988 World Expo, has been transformed into Australia's best urban parkland. There is much to see and do here – dining and shopping facilities to investigate, and visiting the various attractions, which include a man-made beach, the Butterfly and Insect House, weekend markets and, nearby, the **Queensland Maritime Museum**, home of the World War II frigate *Diamantina*.

- ✉ South Brisbane
- ☎ (07) 3867 2051. Maritime Museum: (07) 3844 5361
- 🕐 Daily 8–5. Museum: daily 9:30–5. Museum closed Good Fri, 25 Dec
- ♿ Very good
- 🎫 Free, attractions moderate

Tropical Cairns, the tourism capital of North Queensland, offers a good range of hotels and other facilities

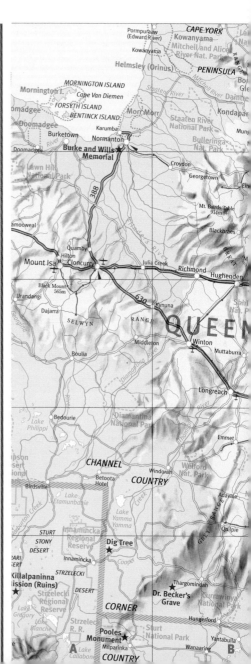

QUEENSLAND

Coral Sea

Starcke National Park
Hope Vale
Cooktown
Lakeland
Rattlesnake Point
Daintree (Cape Tribulation) National Park
Mossman
Daintree
Port Douglas
Mareeba
Cairns
Atherton
1377m
Gordonvale
Wooroonooran (Bellenden Ker)
Garnet
Innisfail   National Park
Ravenshoe
Tully
Cardwell   Rockingham Bay
Lumholtz
Nat. Park
Ingham   GREAT PALM ISLAND
Halifax Bay
MAGNETIC ISLAND
Townsville
Bowling Green Bay National Park
Basalt Wall
Ayr   Cape Upstart
Home   Cape Upstart National Park
Hill   Bowen
Charters Towers   Collinsville   HOOK ISLAND
Pentland   Proserpine   WHITSUNDAY ISLANDS
Cape Conway
White Mountains
National Park
Marian   Mackay
Mount Coolon   Mt. Dalrymple
1259m
Sarina
Nebo   Cape Palmerston
Koumala
Moranbah
Arthur Point
ISLAND
Clermont   North East Point
Dysart   Middlemount   Cape Manifold
Aramac   Capella
Barcaldine   Jericho   578   Emerald   Blackwater
Alpha   Blackdown
Springsure   Tableland
Nat. Park   Yeppoon
Blackall
Rolleston   Rockhampton
Tambo   Consuelo Peak   CURTIS ISLAND
1174m   Mt. Morgan
Moura   Gladstone
Biloela
Augathella   Mt. Hutton   Theodore   Agnes Waters
940m   Miriam Vale
Expedition
Nat. Park   Taroom   Bundaberg
Charleville   Mitchell   Wandoan
Roma   Mundubbera   Great Sandy
(Fraser Island)
National Park
Miles   Mt. Turkey
513m   Gayndah
Indian Head
FRASER ISLAND
Surat   Chinchilla   Gympie
Condamine   Kingaroy   Hervey Bay
Meandarra   Mt. Kiangarow   Maryborough
1135m
Moonie   Dalby   Skip Point
Tin Can Bay
St. George   Millmerran   Nambour
Noosa Heads
Cooloola
National Park
Toowoomba   Caboolture   Sunshine Coast
BRIBIE ISLAND
Goondiwindi   MORETON I.
Beaudesert   BRISBANE
Inglewood   Warwick   Beenleigh   NORTH STRADBROKE ISLAND
Stanthorpe   Killarney   Gold Coast
Wallangarra   Murwillumbah
North Star   Byron Bay
Tenterfield   Ballina   Lennox Head
Moree

GREAT BARRIER REEF

BOUGAINVILLE REEF
FLORA REEF   HOLMES REEFS   WILLIS GROUP
HERALD CAYS
DART
REEF   FLINDERS REEFS   LIHOU REEFS AND CAYS
Hinchinbrook Island National Park
MARION REEF
FREDERIK REEF
SWAIN REEFS
SAUMAREZ REEF

4000
3000
2000
N
0   50   100   150
Kilometres

5
4
3
2
1

The lush farmland of the Atherton Tableland contrasts dramatically with the Cairns coastline

What to See in Queensland

ATHERTON TABLELAND (► 16, TOP TEN)

CARNARVON NATIONAL PARK ★★★

Although it is very remote (over 250km from the nearest town, Roma), a visit to this spectacular park is well rewarded. The Carnarvon Creek has cut through soft sandstone to create 200m cliffs and a 30km-long gorge. There is some good bushwalking, as well as lush vegetation and ancient Aboriginal paintings. Roads may be impassable between January and April.

51C2

⊠ Carnarvon National Park, via Rolleston

☎ (07) 4984 4505

Daily

Roma, then a drive

None Free

CAIRNS AND DISTRICT (► 16, TOP TEN)

CHARTERS TOWERS ★★

Once the second largest city in Queensland, with its own stock exchange, this historic town, situated 130km west of Townsville, was built on gold over a century ago. Today it is a living museum of grand hotels, banks and other National Trust - classified buildings. The World Theatre Foyer, built in 1891 as an international bank, now serves as a focus for arts and entertainment with a fully restored auditorium, cinema, archival center and art gallery. The town has a number of significant events each year, including the Australia Day (26 January) Cricket Festival, the Rodeo (Easter) and one of Australia's largest country music festivals on the May Day weekend. (See also Townsville ► 54).

51C4

Townsville

Townsville

Tourist Information Office: Mosman Street (☎ (07) 4752 0314) Daily 9–5. Closed Good Fri, 25–26 Dec

FRASER ISLAND

At 123km long, this extraordinary World Heritage list inclusion is the world's largest sand island. Yet with extensive rainforest, over 40 freshwater lakes, long sandy beaches, and strangely colored sand cliffs this is a surprisingly varied environment. The wildlife – including dingoes and wallabies – is prolific, making the island the perfect destination for nature lovers and birdwatchers. Fraser Island is reached by vehicular ferry and a four-wheel-drive vehicle is necessary, unless taking one of the many tours.

- 51D2
- From Hervey Bay
- Sunshine Coast (➤ 54)
- Hervey Bay Information Centre: Old Maryborough Road, Hervey Bay
- (☎ (07) 4124 6444) Mon–Sat 8:30–5
- None ■ Free

GOLD COAST (➤ 17, TOP TEN)

GREAT BARRIER REEF (➤ 18–19, TOP TEN)

LAMINGTON NATIONAL PARK

Temperate and subtropical rainforests, wild mountain scenery with waterfalls, gorges, rock pools, caves and abundant wildlife all combine to make this World Heritage-listed national park a must-see destination for nature lovers. There are 160km of hiking tracks to explore, as well

- 51D1
- ✉ O'Reilley's Guesthouse, Green Mountains; Binna Burra Mountain Lodge
- ☎ (07) 5544 0644; (07) 5533 3622
- Daily
- Gold Coast or Brisbane, then a drive
- None ■ Free

as plenty of easy trails and a rainforest canopy trail. The most accessible and popular sections of the national park are Green Mountains and Binna Burra.

LONGREACH ✪

Longreach in Queensland's Outback was the first home of the national airline Qantas (Queensland and Northern Territory Aerial Services) during the 1920s, and the town has many charming old buildings. The major attraction is the excellent **Australian Stockman's Hall of Fame** and Outback Heritage Centre – a modern complex that pays tribute to the early explorers, pioneers and settlers .

MT TAMBORINE (➤ 17, TOP TEN)

World Heritage-listed Fraser Island has long sandy beaches, dunes and unusual sand cliffs

- 50B3
- **Australian Stockman's Hall of Fame**
- ✉ Landsborough Highway
- ☎ (07) 4658 2166
- Longreach
- Daily 9–5. Closed 25 Dec
- Snack bar ($)
- Excellent ■ Expensive

51D1
Nambour, then a bus
To Maroochydore
Brisbane (► 48–9),
Fraser Island (► 53)
Noosa Heads Tourist
Information Centre:
Hastings Street, Noosa
Heads (☎ (07) 5447
4988) ⓘ Daily 9–5.
Closed 25 Dec

SUNSHINE COAST ●●

Stretching for 65km to the north of Brisbane, the Sunshine Coast region has beautiful white beaches, low-key resorts, and some outstanding national parks. The stylish main resort town of **Noosa Heads** offers sandy beaches and cosmopolitan dining, while nearby attractions include cruising the Noosa River, and exploring the dunes and colored sand cliffs of Cooloola National Park. Inland, you can tour the Blackall Range region, where there are green hills, charming villages and rich farming country.

51C4
Townsville
Townsville
Whitsunday Islands
Tourist Information
Centre: Flinders Mall
(☎ (07) 4721 3660)
ⓘ Mon–Fri 9–5, Sat
9–1, Sun 9–12:30

TOWNSVILLE ●●

With a population of almost 140,000, this historic harborside settlement is Australia's largest tropical city. The main points of interest are the excellent Reef HQ aquarium complex, a new museum housing relics from the wreck *HMS Pandora*, the wildlife-rich Billabong Sanctuary, and delightful 19th-century architecture. You can visit nearby Magnetic Island, with its fine beaches and abundant wildlife, and take trips to the Great Barrier Reef.

51C4
**Whitsunday Visitors and
Convention Bureau**
☎ (07) 4946 6673
ⓘ Mon–Fri 9–5
Proserpine

*The glorious Whitsunday
Islands are a haven for
boating enthusiasts*

WHITSUNDAY ISLANDS ●●●

Reached via Proserpine and the villages of Airlie Beach and Shute Harbour, these central coast islands form a very popular holiday destination. There are over 70 islands, mostly hilly and forested, with exquisite beaches and incredibly clear turquoise waters. There is a good choice of resorts – from upmarket Hayman to the less sophisticated national park Long Island resort. There are plenty of day trips to the Reef, and the region is perfect for sailing, snorkeling and other water sports.

From Cairns to the Daintree

This extremely scenic drive takes you beyond the holiday city of Cairns via a scenic coastline to booming Port Douglas and the Daintree's World Heritage rainforest.

From central Cairns, take the Captain Cook Highway north out of town.

Stretching for 30km, the beautiful Marlin Coast has many sandy beaches and small resort villages like Trinity Beach and Palm Cove. Other attractions along the way include the Rainforest Habitat, the Wild World wildlife park and Hartleys Creek Crocodile Farm.

Continue on the Highway, then take the Port Douglas turn-off.

Once a sleepy fishing settlement, charming Port Douglas is now a rather exclusive resort village, with upmarket accommodation, dining and shopping, a picturesque harbor and a perfect, long sandy beach.

Return to the Highway and continue to Mossman.

Mossman has a sugar mill and a few other attractions, but this small town is essentially the gateway to the magnificent Daintree rainforest.

Take the Mossman River Gorge road.

The significance of this lush region – the province of tropical rainforest, many orchid species, the large, flightless cassowary, enormous birdwing butterflies and a rare tree kangaroo – was recognized in 1988, when the Daintree National Park was World Heritage listed. The most easily accessible part of the Daintree is Mossman River Gorge, with its easy 2.7-km circuit hiking trail. Cross the Daintree River on the car ferry and you can take the bitumen road as far as Cape Tribulation (50km). There are several places off this road where you can experience coastal tropical rainforests and white-sand beaches.

Return to Cairns via the same route.

Distance
280km

Time
A full day

Start point
Central Cairns
50B5

End point
Central Cairns
50B5

Lunch
On the Inlet ($)
3 Inlet Street, Port Douglas
(07) 4099 5255

Some of Australia's finest tropical rainforest can be found around Cairns, in the verdant Daintree and Wooroonooran National Parks

Victoria & Tasmania

Australia's most southerly states hold many surprises – a cooler climate (including winter snows) than many would expect, tranquil farmland, rugged peaks, and coastlines lashed by the wild waters of Bass Strait, which divides Victoria from Tasmania.

Victoria, separated from New South Wales by the country's longest river, the Murray, is small and densely populated by Australian standards. From the gracious capital, Melbourne, it is easy to reach attractions that vary from dramatic coastlines to the ski fields and peaks of the Great Dividing Range.

The compact island state of Tasmania is packed with interest. Its violent convict past intrigues history lovers, while the superb coastal, mountain and wilderness scenery provides endless opportunities for outdoor activities. You can fly to Hobart and Launceston from the mainland, or take the *Spirit of Tasmania* ferry from Melbourne.

> '*...a dizzying cocktail of youth, vigour, food and vibrant multiculturalism. Melbournians can turn their dexterous hands to anything.*'
>
> WALLPAPER MAGAZINE
> (January 1999)

Melbourne's ultra-modern Rialto building looms over a 19th-century survivor

The Victorian Arts Centre is capped by its distinctive 115m-high spire, a well-known Melbourne landmark

Melbourne

Australia's second largest city, with a population of around 3 million, Melbourne is very different from its glossy northern sister. Founded long after Sydney, in 1835, this more elegant, European-style city retains many grand buildings and while its citizens are regarded as more conservative than Sydneysiders, this is not borne out in any tangible way. The climate is often 'four seasons in a day' and can be very hot in summer. Melbourne's cooler winter temperatures are often accompanied by romantic, grey days.

Melbourne has plenty to entertain the visitor. There are over 4,000 restaurants and the dining scene is superb; the shopping rivals that of Sydney; sport is practically a religion; and there is plenty of nightlife – including high-quality theatrical and cultural events at the Victorian Arts Centre and other venues.

A vibrant, sophisticated and dynamic city, bisected by the Yarra River (on which you can take a scenic cruise), the central city area contains many museums and galleries, gracious avenues such as Collins and Spring Streets, and an abundance of green open spaces. Another Melbourne delight is riding the extensive tram network; trams have practically disappeared from all other Australian cities, but in Melbourne this is very much the way to get around.

Melbourne is a city of many races and nationalities – as a visit to Chinatown, with its exotic shops and restaurants and the Chinese Museum, or the inner suburbs of Italian-influenced Carlton and multicultural Richmond will reveal. Other enclaves are St Kilda (➤ 60) and South Yarra, with smart boutiques and the grand 1840s house, Como.

Right: A colorful outdoor sculpture marks the entrance of the National Gallery of Victoria

What to See in Melbourne

MELBOURNE CRICKET GROUND ✪✪✪
Visiting this most hallowed of Australia's sporting venues is a must. The city's famous cricket ground, known as the MCG, was the site of the first Australia-England test match in 1877 and the main stadium for the 1956 Olympic Games. Today, the 100,000-capacity ground is used for both cricket and Australian Rules Football, and the complex contains the excellent Olympic and MCG Cricket museums.

✉ Jolimont
☎ (03) 9657 8879
🕐 Daily 9.30–4.30. Closed Good Fri, 25 Dec
🍴 Coffee shop ($)
🚋 Trams 48, 75
♿ Good
⚡ Moderate
❓ Guided tours hourly 10–3 on non event days

MELBOURNE MUSEUM ✪✪✪
When open (mid-2000), this will be the largest museum in the southern hemisphere. The highlights include an Aboriginal Centre, Children's Museum, a living forest gallery, an IMAX theatre and People and Places gallery.

✉ Carlton Gardens, Rathdowne Street
☎ (03) 9651 6777
🚋 Trams 86, 96, City Circle
⚡ Moderate

NATIONAL GALLERY OF VICTORIA ✪✪
The state's most important art gallery (and one of the nation's best) contains some fine examples of Australian colonial and Aboriginal art, as well as a good collection of European works. The gallery is part of the large Victorian Arts Centre complex, which includes a theater and concert halls and an interesting Performing Arts Museum.

✉ 180 St Kilda Road
☎ (03) 9208 0203 or 0220
🕐 Daily 10–5. Closed Good Fri, 25 Dec
🍴 Restaurant ($$)
🚋 Trams 48, 75
♿ Excellent
⚡ Free

OLD MELBOURNE GAOL ✪✪
Although rather grim, this mid-19th century building is nonetheless fascinating. The gaol – the scene of 135 hangings, including that of the notorious bushranger Ned Kelly on 11 November 1880 – provides an idea of what colonial 19th-century prison life was like, and contains many intriguing exhibits, including death masks and a flogging triangle.

✉ Russell Street
☎ (03) 9663 7228
🕐 Daily 9:30–4:30. Closed Good Fri, 25 Dec and Anzac Day AM
🚋 City Circle tram
♿ Few
⚡ Moderate
↔ Queen Victoria Market (► 108)
❓ Atmospheric evening tours available

RIALTO TOWERS OBSERVATION DECK ✪✪✪
The view from this observation deck, on Level 55 of the tallest building in Melbourne, is simply awe-inspiring. The panorama takes in the city and Port Phillip Bay and stretches as far away as the Dandenong Ranges, about 50km from Melbourne.

✉ 525 Collins Street
☎ (03) 9629 8222
🕐 Daily 10AM until late. Closed 25 Dec
🍴 Licensed café ($$)
🚋 City Circle tram
♿ Excellent
⚡ Moderate

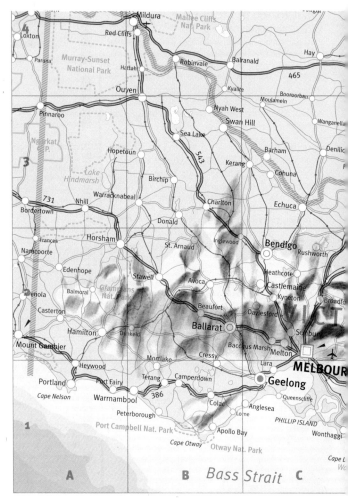

A 4

B

C

465

543

731

386

Mallee Cliffs Nat. Park

Mildura
Red Cliffs
Loxton
Paruna
Murray-Sunset National Park
Hattah
Robinvale
Balranald
Hay
Kyalite
Booroorban
Moulamein
Ouyen
Nyah West
Swan Hill
Wanganella
Pinnaroo
Sea Lake
Barham
Denilic
Ngarkat P.
Hopetoun
Kerang
Cohuna
Lake Hindmarsh
Birchip
Charlton
Echuca
Nhill
Warracknabeal
Bordertown
Donald
Frances
Horsham
St. Arnaud
Inglewood
Bendigo
Rushworth
Naracoorte
Edenhope
Stawell
Grampians Nat. Park
Avoca
Heathcote
Castlemaine
Broadfo
Denola
Balmoral
Beaufort
Kyneton
Casterton
Daylesford
Hamilton
Dunkeld
Ballarat
Sunbur
Heywood
Mortlake
Cressy
Bacchus Marsh
Melton
MELBOUR
Portland
Port Fairy
Terang
Camperdown
Lara
Geelong
Cape Nelson
Warrnambool
Colac
Anglesea
Queenscliffe
Peterborough
Lorne
PHILLIP ISLAND
Port Campbell Nat. Park
Apollo Bay
Wonthaggi
Cape Otway
Otway Nat. Park
Cape L

Mount Gambier

Bass Strait

Right: *The banks of the
Yarra are ideal for rest
and recreation*

ST KILDA   ●●●

Melbourne has many lively suburbs which provide a venue
for Melburnians to let their hair down. Located on the
shores of Port Phillip Bay, St Kilda has been the city's
seaside resort since the 1880s, when the pier was
constructed. Its waterfront pathway is popular with
walkers, cyclists and in-line skaters, and the Luna Park
funfair, built in 1912, continues to be a great attraction.
There are dozens of bustling cafés and restaurants, particularly on Acland Street. The Sunday arts and crafts markets
are good, and you can take a cruise on the bay from the St
Kilda Pier.

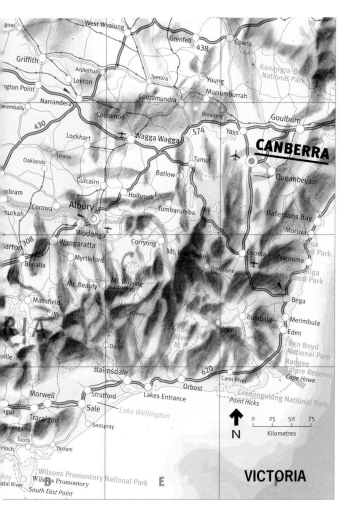

gowl
West Wyalong
Grenfell
438
Cowra
Griffith
Ardlethan
Leeton
Kanangra-Bo
National Park
gton Point
Temora
Young
Narrandera
Cootamundra
Murrumburrah
eambally
430
Codlamon
Binalong
Yass
Goulburn
Lockhart
Wagga Wagga
574
CANBERRA
Oaklands
Urana
Tumut
Queanbeyan
obram
Culcairn
Batlow
murkah
Corowa
Holbrook
Albury
Tumbarumba
Batemans Bay
Moruya
arton
308
Wodonga
Corryong
Cooma
National Park
Wangaratta
Mt. Kosciusko
Narooma
Wadbilliga
Benalla
Myrtleford
Jindabyne
National Park
Mt. Beauty
Mt. Bogong
Justin
Mansfield
Mount;alller
Omeo
Bega
ne
Snow
Bombala
Merimbula
River
Delegate
Eden
Dargo
Ben Boyd
National Park
ville
Nadgee
Bairnsdale
620
Nature Reserve
Cape Howe
Morwell
Stratford
Orbost
Cann River
Croajingolong National Park
agul
Sale
Lakes Entrance
Point Hicks
Traralgon
Lake Wellington
eongatha
Toora
Seaspray
loch
Yarram
Wilsons Promontory National Park
E
VICTORIA
Bay
Wilsons Promontory
dal River
South East Point

0   25   50   75
N
Kilometres

61

Yarra River, Kings Domain & Royal Botanic Gardens

Distance
4 km

Time
2–4 hours, including time for a light lunch

Start point
Flinders Street Station
✚ 60C2
🚋 City Circle tram

End point
Flinders Street Station
✚ 60C2
🚋 City Circle tram

Lunch
Terrace Tearooms ($–$$)
✉ Royal Botanic Gardens
☎ (03) 9820 9590

Facing page: Ballarat's Sovereign Hill historical park faithfully recreates the old goldrush days

The elegant Victorian city of Ballarat features many fine buildings and impressive statues

This walk ventures out beyond Melbourne's city center – along the Yarra River and into the large area of lovely parkland that lies to the south.

Start at Flinders Street Station (corner of Swanston and Flinders Streets), then cross Princes Bridge and turn right for Southbank Promenade.

There are many temptations here in the large Southgate shopping and eating complex. If you can, just admire the view of the city and river from the promenade and continue walking.

Walk under Princes Bridge and follow the path beside the river.

After walking along the Yarra, where you are likely to see many rowing craft, head away from the water at Swan Street Bridge and into the Kings Domain. This lush parkland encompasses impressive Government House, the official residence of the Governor of Victoria.

Continue into the gardens.

The delightful landscaped Royal Botanic Gardens are centered around an extensive ornamental lake. They contain some 60,000 plant species and are one of central Melbourne's most attractive features.

Follow the signs to La Trobe's Cottage.

La Trobe's Cottage, a modest mid-19th-century dwelling, was the home of Charles La Trobe, the state's first governor from 1851 to 1854. It provides a marked contrast to the massive nearby Shrine of Remembrance which contains Victoria's most important war memorial.

From here you can either cross St Kilda Road and take a tram to Flinders Street Station, or walk back via the Kings Domain and call in at the National Gallery of Victoria (➤ 59).

What to See in Victoria

BALLARAT ●●

Gold was discovered near Ballarat in 1851, an event which was to bring incredible wealth to the Victorian colony, and this elegant rural city still contains many grand buildings as a reminder of those boom days. Ballarat's main attraction is the excellent **Sovereign Hill** historical park, a re-creation of life in the gold rush era. Other sights are the Ballarat Wildlife Park and Ballarat Fine Art Gallery.

60C2
Sovereign Hill
✉ Bradshaw Street
☎ (03) 5331 1944
⏰ Daily 10–5. Closed 25 Dec
🍴 Café & restaurant ($–$$)
♿ Good 💷 Expensive

DANDENONG RANGES ●●●

Just 50km east of Melbourne are the delightful Dandenong Ranges – cool, moist hills cloaked with eucalypts and rainforest. Their many attractions include Puffing Billy, a quaint steam train which runs between Belgrave and Gembrook, and the William Ricketts Sanctuary, an unusual park featuring Aboriginal-themed sculptures.

60C2
🚉 Upper Ferntree Gully or Belgrave
ℹ Dandenong Ranges Visitor Information Centre: 1211 Burwood Highway, Ferntree Gully (☎ (03) 9758 7522) ⏰ Daily 9–5. Closed Good Fri, 25 Dec

GREAT OCEAN ROAD (➤ 20, TOP TEN)

PHILLIP ISLAND ●●●

This scenic island, linked by bridge to the mainland, is famous for its nightly Penguin Parade – tiny fairy penguins waddling ashore to their burrows. The site of the parade and its visitor center at Summerland Beach are part of the **Phillip Island Nature Park**, which incorporates the island's **Koala Conservation Centre** (near the main town of Cowes), the ideal place to meet these cuddly marsupials.

60C1
Phillip Island Nature Park
🚌 From Melbourne
♿ Excellent 💷 Moderate
ℹ Visitor Centre & Conservation Centre (☎ (03) 5956 8300)
⏰ Daily 10–5:30

WILSONS PROMONTORY NATIONAL PARK ●●

The spectacular 'Prom' forms the Australian mainland's most southerly point. This is one of Victoria's most popular national parks, offering beaches and superb coastal scenery, rainforests, well-marked hiking tracks, and a wide range of flora and fauna.

61D1
♿ Few 💷 Cheap
ℹ Visitor Centre: Tidal River (☎ (03) 5680 9555)
⏰ Daily from 8:30

This reconstructed 1820s watermill is a central feature of Launceston's Penny Royal World entertainment complex

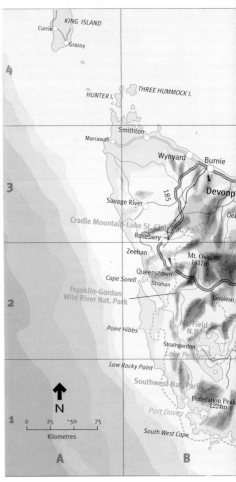

KING ISLAND
Currie
Grassy

4

HUNTER I.   THREE HUMMOCK I.

Smithton
Marrawah
Wynyard   Burnie

3   185   Devonp

Savage River

Cradle Mountain-Lake St. Clair Nat. Park   De

Rosebery

Zeehan   Mt. Ossa
1617m

Queenstown
Cape Sorell   Strahan

Franklin-Gordon
Wild River Nat. Park   Tarraleah

2   Mt. Field
N.P.

Point Hibbs
Strathgordon
Lake Pedder

Low Rocky Point

Southwest Nat. Park

N   Federation Peak
1224m

0   25   50   75   Port Davey

1   Kilometres   South West Cape

A   B

What to See in Hobart

Tasmania's capital is one of Australia's most pleasant settlements. The small city of Hobart, on the River Derwent, is full of old colonial buildings; walking is the best way to appreciate the historic atmosphere. While here, you should take a river cruise and a trip to the top of Mount Wellington (1,270m), which dominates the city – the view is sensational.

Left: The attractive city of Hobart is dominated by the vast bulk of 1,270m-high Mount Wellington

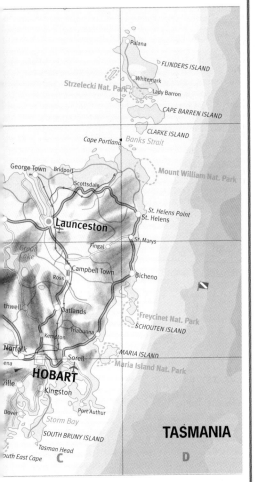

Tasmania, Australia's most 'English' state, is full of charming old buildings

Maritime Museum
- ⊠ Secheron Road
- ☎ (03) 6223 5082
- 🕐 Daily 10–4:30. Closed Good Fri, 25 Dec
- ♿ Few
- 🖐 Cheap

- ⊠ Queens Domain
- ☎ (03) 6234 6299
- 🕐 Daily from 8
- 🍴 Restaurant ($$)
- ♿ Good
- 🖐 Free

- ⊠ Salamanca Place
- 🕐 Markets: Sat 9–3
- 🍴 Many cafés and restaurants ($–$$$)
- ♿ Few
- 🖐 Free

- ⊠ 40 Macquarie Street
- ☎ (03) 6235 0777
- 🕐 Daily 10–5. Closed Good Fri, 25 Dec and Anzac Day
- ♿ Excellent 🖐 Free

- ✚ 65D2
- 🚌 Bicheno or Coles Bay
- ℹ Information Centre, Tasman Highway, Bicheno (☎ (03) 6375 1333) 🕐 Daily 9–5

- ✚ 65C3
- 🚍 Launceston
- ✈ Launceston
- ℹ Tasmanian Travel and Information Centre: Cnr St John/Paterson Streets (☎ (03) 6336 3122) 🕐 Mon–Fri 9–5, Sat 9–3, Sun (summer only) 9–12

66

BATTERY POINT ✪✪✪

With its charming mid-19th-century cottages and houses, craft and antiques shops and quaint streets like Arthur's Circus, this inner city 'village' is Hobart's showpiece. Highlights are the excellent **Maritime Museum of Tasmania**, in a grand 1830s house, the Van Diemen's Land Folk Museum, and the 1818 Signal Station and military base from which the suburb takes its name.

ROYAL TASMANIAN BOTANICAL GARDENS ✪✪

These gardens, set high overlooking the river and full of native and exotic plants, form part of the large area of parkland known as the **Queens Domain**. They include a Conservatory, a Tropical Glasshouse and a museum of botany and horticulture.

SALAMANCA PLACE ✪✪✪

This delightful old dockside street is lined with sandstone warehouses converted into restaurants and arts and crafts shops, and is the venue for Hobart's lively Saturday market (► 108). Stroll around nearby Sullivans Cove – where the first settlers landed in 1804 – to see Constitution and Victoria Docks, historic Hunter Street and Tasmania's 1840 Parliament House.

TASMANIAN MUSEUM AND ART GALLERY ✪✪✪

Hobart's Tasmanian Museum contains some fine and varied exhibits, particularly on Australian mammals, convict history and Tasmanian Aborigines. The attached art gallery holds a good collection of colonial art. This is an ideal place to start discovering the history of the island.

What to See in Tasmania

FREYCINET PENINSULA ✪✪✪

Tasmania's east coast is renowned for beautiful scenery, none of which surpasses that of **Freycinet National Park** with its sandy white beaches and abundance of flora, birds and animals. The park is reached via the fishing settlement of Coles Bay, and the town of Bicheno has yet more excellent beaches, great diving, a sealife center and a wildlife park.

LAUNCESTON ✪✪

Tasmania's second city, sited on the Tamar River and founded in 1805 (a year after Hobart), has retained many of its old buildings, which can be viewed on a self-guided walk around town. There are pleasant parks and reserves – a visit to the spectacular Cataract Gorge reserve is recommended. The Queen Victoria Museum is interesting, and the Penny Royal World amusement park is great fun for families. The Launceston region is rich in historic houses and wineries.

THE MIDLANDS ✪

The Midlands Highway, running for 200km between Hobart and Launceston, passes through charming and historic towns. Oatlands is full of atmospheric old buildings such as the Court House, while, further north, picturesque Ross is famous for its 1836 bridge and contains the **Tasmanian Wool Centre**, devoted to the state's extensive wool industry.

🚩 65C2
Tasmanian Wool Centre
✉ Church Street, Ross
☎ (03) 6381 5466
🕐 Daily, generally 9–5
🚌 Tigerline from Hobart
♿ Good
💰 Cheap

PORT ARTHUR AND THE TASMAN PENINSULA ✪✪✪

Established as a far-flung penal settlement for the worst convict offenders in 1830, Port Arthur has over 30 ruins and historic sites, an excellent museum, and the settlement's poignant burial ground, the Isle of the Dead.

The surrounding Tasman Peninsula has magnificent scenery on the east coast, the Tasmanian Devil Park with an excellent wildlife collection, and the scenic Bush Mill Steam Railway.

🚩 65C1
✉ Port Arthur Historic Site
☎ (03) 6250 2363
🕐 Daily 9–5
🚌 Tigerline from Hobart
♿ Excellent
💰 Moderate
❓ Admission fee includes cruise and guided walk

STRAHAN ✪✪

The lightly populated west coast is a region of wild coastline, rivers and forest lands. From the waterside village of Strahan (pronounced 'Strawn') you can go fishing, take a scenic flight, and cruise Macquarie Harbour – once the site of the brutal Sarah Island penal settlement – and the pristine Gordon River, part of the World Heritage-listed Franklin-Gordon Wild Rivers National Park. In town, the **Strahan Wharf Centre** provides a fascinating lesson in local history.

🚩 64B2
Strahan Wharf Centre
✉ The Esplanade
☎ (03) 6471 7488
🕐 Daily: 10–5 winter, 10–8 summer. Closed 25 Dec
🍽 Café ($)
🚌 Strahan 🚌 Strahan
♿ Good 💰 Cheap

TASMANIA'S WORLD HERITAGE AREA (▶ 25, TOP TEN)

Hobart is delightfully set on the River Derwent

67

In the Know

If your time in Australia is limited, or you would like to get a real flavor of the country, here are some ideas:

10
Ways To Be A Local

Change your accent – to sound like a real Aussie, draw out the vowels, so that, for example, 'park' becomes 'pahk'.

Relax, Australia is not the place to go in for excessive formality, and 'no worries' is not a popular expression for nothing.

Use 'g'day' instead of 'hello', and call virtually everyone 'mate'.

Wear a hat, not just for fashion, but as a necessity to avoid the sun's harmful rays.

Head for an Aussie pub or two to sample the excellent local beers and wines.

Learn the basic facts about convict, colonial and Aboriginal history, and remember that racist jokes are in extremely bad taste.

Spend most of your time outdoors, particularly on the beach or bushwalking.

The Melbourne Cricket Ground holds 100,000 spectators

Dress casually – summer shorts and sandals are acceptable in nearly all places.

Go to a cricket match, or an Aussie Rules football game in winter, to soak up the atmosphere of the national sports.

Get invited to an Aussie barbecue, where you will enjoy a relaxed meal and a unique cultural experience.

10
Good Places To Have Lunch

Blakes ($$), GR2, Southgate, Southbank, Melbourne (☎ (03) 9699 4100). Great Modern Australian cuisine right on the Yarra River.

Boltz Café & Bar ($), 286 Rundle Street, Adelaide (☎ (08) 8232 5234). Good-value food in the heart of Adelaide's shopping center.

City Gardens Café ($–$$), City Botanic Gardens, Brisbane (☎ (07) 3229 1554). Good lunchtime fare in a delightful location.

Doyle's on the Beach ($$), 11 Marine Parade, Watsons Bay, Sydney (☎ (02) 9337 2007). Fine seafood with wonderful harbor views.

Fraser's ($$), Fraser Avenue, Kings Park, Perth (☎ (08) 9481 7100). Modern Australian dining in Perth's famous parklands.

Hyde Park Barracks Café ($–$$), Queens Square, Macquarie Street, Sydney (☎ (02) 9223 1155). A smart city-center café with outdoor tables.

Il Bacaro ($$), 168–170 Little Collins Street, Melbourne (☎ (03) 9654 6778). Highly recommended Italian food in Melbourne's city center.

Mures Upper Deck ($$), Mures Fish Centre, Victoria Dock, Hobart (☎ (03) 6231 1999). A great seafood menu in the perfect waterfront spot.

Satay King ($), Galleria Complex, The Mall, Darwin (☎ (08) 8981 3362). Superb city-center Asian soups and satays.

Tu Tu Tango ($$), 124 Bunda Street, Canberra City (☎ (02) 6257 7100). Take a break in Canberra at this southwest American restaurant.

10
Top Activities

Boating: sail a yacht around Queensland's Whitsunday Islands, or rent a houseboat on the Murray River.

Bushwalking: there are countless places to go hiking, but try Tasmania and the Blue Mountains near Sydney.

Cross-country skiing: the conditions are ideal around the ski fields of Victoria, Tasmania and New South Wales.

Fishing: from trout fishing in Tasmania's lakes to big-game marlin wrestling off Cairns.

Four-wheel-driving adventures: the Pinnacles in WA is an ideal venue.

Golf: in Australia golf is a sport for everyone. There are excellent courses everywhere, but those on the Gold Coast are particularly recommended.

Horse riding: the south-east is ideal – around the Snowy Mountains of NSW and Victoria's alpine areas.

Scuba diving and snorkeling: there is nowhere better than along the Great Barrier Reef.

Surfing: the quintessential Aussie sport – Sydney's coastline, Bells Beach in Victoria and Margaret River in the west are all good spots.

Tennis: you will find day/night courts in every major city.

5
Great Views

- From the AMP Tower, Sydney.
- Brisbane – from the lookout at Mt Coot-tha.
- From Mount Wellington, Hobart.
- From Rialto Towers Observation Deck, Melbourne.
- From Telstra Tower on Black Mountain, Canberra.

5
Exceptional Lesser Known Destinations

- Bathurst and Melville Islands, Northern Territory: the home of the indigenous Tiwi people and their traditional culture.
- Coober Pedy, South Australia: an opal mining town with most buildings underground.
- Jervis Bay, New South Wales: white sands, clear blue waters and unspoilt bushland.
- Ningaloo Reef, near Exmouth, Western Australia: the diving here rivals that of the Great Barrier Reef.
- Magnetic Island, near Townsville in north Queensland: rocky headlands, secluded bays and friendly locals.

Boating is very popular around the long coastline

South Australia & Northern Territory

Founded in 1836 and settled mostly by non-convicts, South Australia has an extraordinary range of scenery. There are fertile farming lands in the south, but the vast majority of the land is taken up by the arid deserts and peaks of the Outback. The state is vast, and has many attractions other than those included here, such as the remote opal mining town of Coober Pedy.

Originally part of South Australia, the sparsely populated Northern Territory is still real frontier country. Almost half of the population, a large proportion of which are Aboriginal people, lives in cosmopolitan Darwin. From the tropical 'Top End' to the desert lands of the 'Red Centre' around Alice Springs, the Northern Territory is endlessly fascinating, with superb natural attractions like Kakadu and Uluru (Ayers Rock).

> *'It's so empty and featureless, like a newspaper that has been entirely censored. We used to drive for miles, always expecting that around the next corner there'd be something to look at, but there never was. That is the charm of Australia.'*

ROBERT MORLEY
on Australia's Outback (1949)

Waterfall, Kakadu National Park

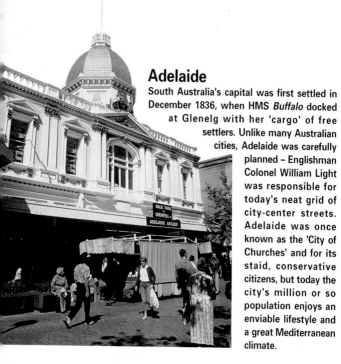

Adelaide

South Australia's capital was first settled in December 1836, when HMS *Buffalo* docked at Glenelg with her 'cargo' of free settlers. Unlike many Australian cities, Adelaide was carefully planned – Englishman Colonel William Light was responsible for today's neat grid of city-center streets. Adelaide was once known as the 'City of Churches' and for its staid, conservative citizens, but today the city's million or so population enjoys an enviable lifestyle and a great Mediterranean climate.

A street in Adelaide – the capital of South Australia and one of the nation's most pleasant cities

Surrounded by large areas of parkland, and with the Adelaide Hills forming a splendid backdrop, Adelaide's compact and mostly flat city center is a delightful place to explore; there are many old buildings, relatively little traffic, and a sense of calm which is rare in urban environments. This elegant city is famous for its café and restaurant scene, as well as for a thriving artistic and cultural life. The ideal time to be here is during the biennial (every even-numbered year), internationally acclaimed Adelaide Festival of Arts, when the city comes alive with everything from classical music concerts to outrageous fringe theatre.

In addition to visiting the museums and attractions detailed below, you should take a cruise on the placid and scenic River Torrens, which passes through the city. Within the metropolitan area, you can also visit the charming seaside suburb of Glenelg, where the first settlers landed in 1836 – it can be reached by an enjoyable tram ride from the city center. The historic settlement of Port Adelaide was once the city's harbor town, but now concentrates on its heritage attractions, including the well presented South Australian Maritime Museum (➤ 111) and the Port Dock Station railway museum complex, the largest of its kind in the country.

What to See in Adelaide

ART GALLERY OF SOUTH AUSTRALIA AND NORTH TERRACE ✪✪✪

A stroll down North Terrace, Adelaide's grandest avenue, is the best way to see the city's historic buildings, several of which are open to the public. At the western end are the Adelaide Casino in a restored 1920s railway station, Old Parliament House, and the latter's neighboring, much more impressive successor. East of King William Street lie the South Australian Museum, the Art Gallery of South Australia, and 1840s Ayers House, former home of Sir Henry Ayers, who was seven times Premier of South Australia and the inspiration behind the naming of Ayers Rock.

✉ Art Gallery of South Australia: North Terrace
☎ (08) 8207 7000
🕐 Daily 10–5. Closed Good Fri AM, 25 Dec
🍽 Café ($)
🚌 City Loop or 99B
♿ Good
🏷 Free
❓ Free guided tours at regular intervals.

GLENELG ✪✪

Take the vintage tram from Victoria Square in the city to this popular seaside suburb where you can soak up the history and have a relaxed lunch in one of the many excellent eating establishments. Walk the pier and be sure to check out the replica of the HMS *Buffalo*, where there is an interesting museum and a top seafood restaurant.

🚌 Glenelg tram or 99B
♿ Good
🏷 Free

SOUTH AUSTRALIAN MUSEUM ✪✪✪

In addition to the usual natural history and general ethnographic and anthropological displays, this better-than-average museum has an internationally acclaimed collection of Aboriginal Australian artefacts. Another highlight is the large Melanesian exhibit.

✉ North Terrace
☎ (08) 8207 7500
🕐 Daily 10–5. Closed Good Fri, 25 Dec
♿ Good
🏷 Free

TANDANYA ABORIGINAL CULTURAL INSTITUTE ✪✪✪

This illuminating center is the only Aboriginal venture of its kind in Australia. Including galleries with high-quality changing art exhibitions, workshops, and an area for dance and other performing arts, Tandanya (the local Aboriginal name for the Adelaide region) is a must for visitors. The center has a shop selling gifts and a variety of good Aboriginal-made items.

✉ 253 Grenfell Street
☎ (08) 8223 2467
🕐 Daily 10–5
🚌 City Loop
♿ Good
🏷 Cheap
↔ Adelaide Botanic Gardens and Adelaide Zoo (▶ 76) Art Gallery of SA/North Terrace (see above)

Shop for high-quality Aboriginal arts and crafts at Adelaide's Tandanya Cultural Institute

73

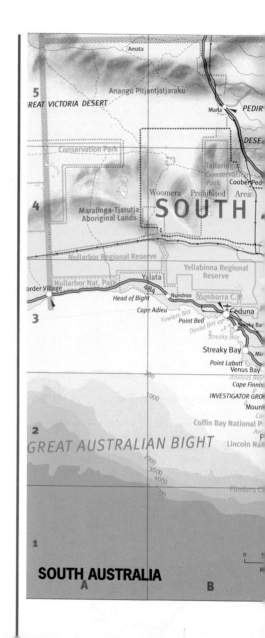

SOUTH AUSTRALIA

Birdsville

Simpson Desert
Conservation Park

*Vitjira
Nat. Park*

Lake
Etamunbanie

Pandie

Macumba River

Simpson Desert
Regional Reserve

STURT
STONY
DESERT

Innamincka
Regional Reserve

Dig Tree

Oodnadatta

Innamincka

TIRARI
DESERT

Giles Memorial ★

Lake Eyre
North
National Park

Lake Eyre

STRZELECKI
DESERT

Killalpaninna
Mission (Ruins) ★

*ake
wirroeoma*

Elliot Price
C.P.

Strzelecki
Regional
Reserve

Lake
Gregory

Lake
Blanche

Strzelecki
R.R.

*Lake
Eyre South*

River

AUSTRALIA

Marree

Lake
Callabonna

Pooles
Monumer

Roxby Downs

Benbonnathe Hill
1064m

*Lake
Frome*

Lake Fron
Regional
Park

Lake

Woomera

Torrens
(Salt)

Lake Torrens
National Park

*arnpon anges
ational Parks*

Fowlers Gap

*Lake
Gairdner*

Lake Gairdner
National Park

Flinders Ranges
National Park

*Lake
Macfarlane*

Hawker

Mt Plantagenet
952m

Broken Hill

AWLER RANGE

776

Port Augusta

Quorn

Cockburn

Olary

Danggali
Conservatio
Park

Coombah

ra

Iron Knob

Yunta

270

Orroroo

Wudinna

Whyalla

Port Pirie

Peterborough

Jamestown

247

Chowilla
Reg. Res.

Kimba

Crystal Brook

Burra

Coombah

Wentwor

Lock

Cowell

Port Broughton

Morgan

Waikerie

399

Renmark

Tooligie

Wallaroo

Moonta

Clare

Eudunda

Murray
Sunset
tional Pa

ston

Ungarra

Balaklava

Nuriootpa

Barmera

Loxton

Paruna

Cummins

*Spencer
Gulf*

*SIR JOSEPH
BANKS GROUP*

Hamley Bridge

Minlaton

Gulf

Gawler

Alawoona

colm

Yorktown

ADELAIDE

St Vincen

Mannum

West Point

Hahndorf

Murray Bridge

Innes Nat. Park

Victor Harbor

Tailem Bend

Pinnaroo

Coomandook

KANGAROO ISLAND Kingscote

Vennachar Point Pandana

Goolwa

Ngar

*Lake
Hindmars*

*ational Park
Maupertuis Bay*

American River

Coonalpyn

Keith

Nhill

Cape Du Couedic

Seal Bay

Coorong
National Park

Lacepede Bay

Bordertown

Padthaway

731

418

France

Naracoorte

00   150

Kingston SE

Cape Jaffa

es

Robe

Horsham

Edenhop

Penola

Lucindale

Balmoral

C

Cape Rebelais

Millicent

Mount Gambier

Casterton

Hamiffon

Port MacDonnell

Heywoo

*The Murray River, once
the domain of paddle
steamers, is now a
popular place for
houseboating holidays*

North Adelaide & City Parklands

Distance
2km

Time
2–4 hours, depending on time at the zoo and in the gardens

Start point
Adelaide Festival Centre
✚ 75C2
🚌 99B or 222

End point
North Terrace
✚ 75C2
🚌 99B

Lunch
The Oxford ($$)
✉ 101 O'Connell Street, North Adelaide
☎ (08) 8267 2652

An easy walk which takes you beyond the city center and into some of Adelaide's delightful parklands.

Start on King William Road, just beyond the junction with North Terrace.

Adelaide Festival Centre is the heart of Adelaide's arts scene. The large modern building houses several performance halls, and a lively market is held outside on Sundays. River cruises start in front of the center.

Continue north on King William Road, crossing the River Torrens on Adelaide Bridge.

St Peter's Cathedral dates from 1859; the bells are the heaviest and finest in the southern hemisphere.

Walk along Pennington Terrace to reach Montefiore Hill.

From the look-out, 'Light's Vision', next to the statue of Colonel William Light, there are wonderful views.

Walk up Jeffcott Street towards Wellington Square, then turn right at Archer Street to reach O'Connell Street.

The elegant suburb of North Adelaide contains many grand old homes. A lively pub, café and gallery scene thrives along O'Connell and Melbourne Streets.

From O'Connell Street, turn left into Brougham Place, then right into Frome Road to reach Melbourne Street. Return to Frome Road and cross the River Torrens via Albert Bridge to Adelaide's small zoo.

Adelaide Zoo is one of Australia's oldest. It has good aviaries and reptile house and an entertaining collection of Australian mammals.

Follow the signs to the Botanic Gardens.

The spacious Adelaide Botanic Gardens are delightful. Don't miss the Palm House and the Bicentennial Conservatory, a vast glass dome containing a tropical rainforest.

Return to North Terrace.

The plaza of the Adelaide Festival Centre features some unusual, brightly colored sculptures

What to See in South Australia

ADELAIDE HILLS ✪✪

Just 20 minutes east of the city, this region of hills, bushland, vineyards and interesting small towns is a popular weekend destination. Attractions include good views from the summit of Mount Lofty, botanic gardens, the acclaimed National Motor Museum at Birdwood, and Warrawong Sanctuary – an important wildlife reserve. The picturesque main town of **Hahndorf** has fine artworks in the Hahndorf Academy.

75D2
From Adelaide
Barossa Valley (see below)
Tourist Information Centre: 41 Main Street, Hahndorf (08) 8388 1185) Daily 10–4. Closed 25 Dec

BAROSSA VALLEY ✪✪✪

The wine-producing area of the Barossa was settled in the 1830s by Silesians and Prussians, and this picturesque valley is characterized by distinctive European architecture, traditions and cuisine. You can visit some of the 45 or so wineries to sample the fine wines and brandies, and enjoy the ambience of towns like Tanunda, Bethany, Lyndoch and Angaston.

75D2
From Adelaide
Adelaide Hills (see above), Murray Riverlands (see below)
Barossa Wine and Visitor Centre: 66–68 Murray Street, Tanunda (08) 8563 0600; fax (08) 8563 0616) Daily 10–4. Closed Good Fri, 25 Dec

COOBER PEDY (➤ 69)

COONAWARRA REGION (➤ PANEL BELOW)

FLINDERS RANGES NATIONAL PARK ✪✪

A rugged desert mountain chain containing one of the most ancient landscapes on earth. Plenty of wildlife can be found, while there are several good hikes that allow you to see the diverse plantlife. The highlights of the Park are Wilpena Pound, an enormous 80-sq km elevated amphitheater surrounded by sheer cliffs, and St Mary's Peak (1,165m), a challenging walk for experienced hikers. The area features abundant Aboriginal art.

75D3
From Adelaide
Wadlata Outback Centre: 41 Flinders Tce, Port Augusta (08) 8641 0793) Mon–Fri 9–5.30, Sat & Sun 10–4. Closed Good Fri, 25 Dec

KANGAROO ISLAND ✪✪✪

Australia's third largest island is a relaxed place with spectacular scenery, remarkable wildlife, and pleasant small towns like the main settlement of Kingscote. There are rugged cliffs and sandy beaches; a large part of the island is within Flinders Chase National Park, domain of kangaroos, koalas and prolific birdlife; and you can view Australian sea lions from close quarters at Seal Bay Conservation Park.

75C1
From Adelaide
From Glenelg or Cape Jervis
Tourism Kangaroo Island: Howard Drive, Penneshaw (08) 8553 1185) Daily

Did you know?

Although the Barossa Valley is South Australia's most famous wine area, the Clare Valley further north, the Coonawarra region in the southeast, and McLaren Vale, south of Adelaide, also produce fine wines. Some of the best wineries in these areas are Tim Knappstein Wines at Clare, Penfolds at Coonawarra, and Hardy's McLaren Vale.

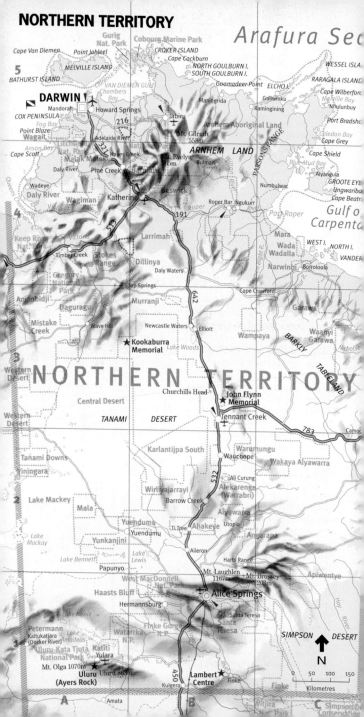

NORTHERN TERRITORY

Arafura Sea

Gurig
Nat. Park
Cobourg Marine Park
Cape Van Diemen
Point Jahleel
CROKER ISLAND
Cape Cockburn
NORTH GOULBURN I.
WESSEL ISLA
MELVILLE ISLAND
SOUTH GOULBURN I.
RARAGALA ISLAND
BATHURST ISLAND
Goomadeer Point
ELCHO I.
Cape Wilberforce
Melville Bay
Maningrida
Ramingining
Galiwinku
Nhulunbuy
DARWIN
Mandorah
Howard Springs
Jabiru
Port Bradshaw
COX PENINSULA
216
Arnhem Aboriginal Land
Caledon Bay
Fog Bay
Point Blaze
Adelaide River
Mt Gilruth
Cape Grey
Wagait
558m
Anson Bay
Hayes Creek
ARNHEM LAND
Cape Shield
Cape Scott
321
Mt Evelyn
Blue Mud Bay
Malak Malak
Pine Creek
Bulman
Nat. Park
Daly River
Beswick
Numbulwar
Wadeye
Katherine
Roper Bar
Ngukurr
GROOTE EYL
Daly River
191
Roper
River
Pt Roper
Ungwariba
Wagiman
Cape Beatri
Keep River
Nat.
Larrimah
Mara
WEST I.
NORTH I.
VANDER
Timber Creek
Stokes
Dillinya
Wada
Wadalla
Narwinbi
Borroloola
Range
Daly Waters
Gregory
National
Park
Top Springs
642
Cape Crawford
Garawa
Amanbidji
Murranji
BARKLY
Waanyi
Garawa
Dagaragu
Newcastle Waters
Elliott
Wampaya
Mistake
Creek
Wave Hill
Kookaburra
Memorial
Lake Woods
TABLELAND
Nicholso
Western
Desert
NORTHERN
TERRITORY
Churchills Head
John Flynn
Memorial
Central Desert
Tennant Creek
Western
Desert
TANAMI
DESERT
783
Camoo
Karlantijpa South
Warumungu
Wauchope
Tanami Downs
Ali Curung
Yiningara
Lake Mackey
532
Alekarenge
(Warrabri)
Wirliyajarrayi
Mala
Barrow Creek
Alyawarra
Yuendumu
Yuendumu
Ti Tree
Ahakeye
Utopia
Angarapa
Yunkanjini
Aileron
Lake
Bennett
Lake
Lewis
Papunyo
Harts Range
West MacDonnell Nat. Park
Mt Laughlen
1167m
Mt Brossey
1208m
Apiwentye
Haasts Bluff
Alice Springs
Hermannsburg
Santa Teresa
Petermann
Kaltukatjara
(Docker River)
Lake
Amadeus
Finke Gorge
N.P.
Santa
Teresa
SIMPSON
DESERT
Uluru-Kata Tjuta
National Park
Watarrka
N.P.
Yulara
Kaititi
Mt. Olga 1070m
Uluru 865m
450
Uluru
(Ayers Rock)
Kulgera
Lambert
Centre
Finke
Finke
Mt Olga
N
0   50   100   150
Kilometres
Amata
Witjira
Nat. Park
Simpson
Conservatio

A   B   C

Darwin

The Northern Territory's capital and largest city, with a multiracial population of about 85,000, was founded in 1869. Bombed by the Japanese during World War II, Darwin suffered another catastrophe in 1974, when Cyclone Tracy virtually flattened the city. Located on vast Darwin Harbour (on which a cruise is highly recommended), this tropical, modern settlement is a laid-back place. Few reminders of Darwin's history remain, but you can visit the 1883 Fannie Bay Gaol and take a historical walk around the city center.

Mindil Beach is the ideal spot to view Darwin's often spectacular tropical sunsets

DARWIN BOTANIC GARDENS ✪✪
Containing the southern hemisphere's most extensive collection of tropical palms, an orchid farm, a rainforest area and wetlands flora, Darwin's gardens are a delightful place in which to relax or escape the heat.

✉ Gardens Road
☎ (08) 8981 1958
🕐 Daily 7AM–7PM
♿ Good
🎫 Free

DARWIN WHARF PRECINCT ✪✪✪
This busy waterfront complex includes shops, cafés and restaurants, and you can go fishing or take a boat excursion from the wharf. The Australian Pearling Exhibition is here, as are the Indo Pacific Marine – an award-winning education and environment center – and the Deckchair Outdoor Cinema.

✉ Stokes Hill Wharf
☎ (08) 8981 4268
🕐 Daily, attractions 10–5
♿ Good
🎫 Moderate (for attractions)

MINDIL BEACH ✪✪
Although swimming is not recommended between October and May (due to box jellyfish), this pleasant beach offers a park, wonderful sunsets, Darwin's casino, and the famous **Mindil Beach Markets** (➤ 108).

Mindil Beach Markets
☎ (08) 8981 3454
🕐 Apr–Oct Thu 5–10,
May– Aug Sun 4–9

MUSEUM AND ART GALLERY OF THE NORTHERN TERRITORY ✪✪✪
This well-planned, modern complex includes the Maritime Museum, a good collection of Aboriginal and Australian art, and displays on local and military history, natural science and Cyclone Tracy. There is a café in the museum.

✉ Conacher St, Bullocky Point
☎ (08) 8999 8201
🕐 Daily. Closed Good Fri,
25 Dec
♿ Excellent
🎫 Free

79

What to See in the Northern Territory

ALICE SPRINGS ✪✪✪

Affectionately known as 'The Alice', this unpretentious Outback town at the heart of the continent was founded as a remote Overland Telegraph station in 1871. Alice Springs is full of attractions: you can take a camel ride, or visit the Old Telegraph Station, the Royal Flying Doctor Service base, a variety of museums and the Strehlow Research Centre, focusing on Aboriginal history and culture. Nearby, the rugged MacDonnell Ranges contain steep gorges, nature reserves, historic settlements and homesteads, ancient Aboriginal sites, national parks, and Palm Valley, where 3,000 rare and ancient palm trees grow.

🚩 78B1
🚊 The Ghan from Adelaide and Sydney
❌ Alice Springs
ℹ Central Australian Tourism Industry Association: Centrepoint Building, Corner Gregory Terrace and Hartley Street (☎ (08) 8952 5800; fax (08) 8953 0295) 🕐 Mon–Fri 9–6, Sat–Sun 9–4

An old aircraft of the renowned Royal Flying Doctor Service

🚩 78B3
ℹ Tennant Creek Tourist Association: Transit Centre (☎ (08) 8962 3388) 🕐 Mon–Fri 9–5, Sat 9–12. Closed Good Fri, 25 Dec

DEVIL'S MARBLES ✪✪

Beside the Stuart Highway to the south of Tennant Creek, these huge, curiously eroded granite boulders are significant in Aboriginal mythology – legend says they are the eggs of the Rainbow Serpent.

KAKADU NATIONAL PARK (➤ 21, TOP TEN)

KATHERINE AND NITMILUK NATIONAL PARK ✪✪

Katherine, the Territory's third largest settlement, is a pleasant town with a museum, a nature reserve and some historic buildings. The main attraction is nearby Nitmiluk (Katherine Gorge) National Park, containing 13 dramatic sandstone gorges. The best way to appreciate Nitmiluk is by taking a cruise on the Katherine River.

🚩 78B4
❌ Katherine
ℹ Katherine Regional Tourist Association: Lindsay Street (☎ (08) 8972 2650) 🕐 Mon–Fri 8:45–5, Sat 9–3, Sun (May–Sep only) 9–3. Closed Good Fri, 25 Dec.

ULURU–KATA TJUTA NATIONAL PARK (➤ 26, TOP TEN)

WATARRKA NATIONAL PARK ✪✪

This remote, rugged desert park, north of Uluru, is famous for Kings Canyon – a spectacular sandstone gorge with walls almost 300m high. Visitors can explore lush waterholes, wonder at the strangely weathered rocks of the Lost City, and take a challenging bushwalk. There is a wide variety of flora and fauna, including some extraordinary ancient palm trees.

🚩 78A1
🚊 None
♿ Few 💳 Free
ℹ Central Australian Tourism Industry Association, Alice Springs (see above)

Darwin to Litchfield National Park

This drive makes an easy day trip, and the itinerary takes in several fun attractions outside Darwin, plus a superb national park.

From Darwin's center, follow the signs to the Stuart Highway and Winnellie.

In the outer suburb of Winnellie, the Australian Aviation Heritage Centre has a good collection of aircraft, including a massive B-52 bomber.

Continue south on the Highway.

Darwin Crocodile Farm, 40km south of Darwin, has over 8,000 saltwater and freshwater crocodiles. This farm and research center is the ideal place to inspect the most fearsome of reptiles.

Continue south, then take the Berry Springs turn-off.

Berry Springs has two major attractions – the large Territory Wildlife Park, with its excellent collection of native fauna, and the nearby Berry Springs Nature Park, a great spot for a swim or a barbecue.

Return to the Stuart Highway and drive south. Take the Batchelor turn-off.

The small settlement of Batchelor, once a dormitory town for workers at the nearby Rum Jungle uranium field, is best known as the gateway to Litchfield National Park.

Continue for another 21km into the park.

Litchfield National Park, a rugged yet delightful reserve, was little known before the mid-1980s, as it was on private land. Nowadays, the many visitors come to enjoy the four spectacular waterfalls, refreshing swimming holes, hiking trails, and superb views of the surrounding region. Other highlights are a small 1930s pioneers' homestead; tall 'magnetic' termite mounds, so called because they always face north–south; and the Lost City, an area of curious sandstone pillars.

Return to Darwin via Batchelor and the Stuart Highway.

Distance
280km

Time
A full day is necessary

Start point
Central Darwin
✚ 78A5

End point
Central Darwin
✚ 78A5

Lunch
Territory Wildlife Park (kiosk only) ($)
✉ Cox Peninsula Road, Berry Springs
☎ (08) 8988 6000

Spring-fed waterfalls are a highlight of Litchfield National Park, a pleasant drive south of Darwin

Western Australia

Western Australia takes up almost a third of the continent, but is home to only 1.2 million people, the vast majority living in Perth and its port, Fremantle. Much of the terrain is arid and used for little more than cattle farming and mining. The discovery of gold in the southeast in the 1890s initially brought prosperity, and modern Western Australia has boomed because of the extraordinary wealth created by iron ore mining in particular.

Natural wonders here are remarkable: tall forests in the southwest; a coastline of white sandy beaches and rugged cliffs; extraordinary wildlife, including marsupials like the numbat and quokka, unique to the state; and the dramatic rock formations of the Kimberley in the far north. Many of the glorious southern wild flowers are also found nowhere else in Australia. Although there is much to see here, remember that distances are vast – flying is the best option for getting around.

> *'An ingenious but sarcastic Yank, when asked what he thought of WA, declared that it was the best country he had ever seen to run through an hour-glass.'*

ANTHONY TROLLOPE
Australia & New Zealand (1873)

The Pinnacles, Nambung National Park

The modern city of Perth provides an enviable lifestyle, centered around its beaches and the delightful Swan River

Perth

Founded in 1829 by free settlers, and initially known as the Swan River Colony, Perth began life as an incredibly isolated outpost of Sydney and the eastern part of the continent. This isolation continues today. Despite its prosperity and cosmopolitan ambience, Perth is the world's most remote city – separated from the east by the desert lands of the Nullarbor Plain, with the nearest large center, Adelaide, over 2,700km away.

Much of Perth's charm is due to its location. The city is in a delightful setting on the broad Swan River; some of Australia's best urban beaches lie to the west; and the metropolitan area is backed by the low hills of the Darling Ranges to the east. The climate is warm and sunny, the generally rather affluent lifestyle is enviable, and the atmosphere is as relaxed as that of any capital city.

Perth's small and mostly modern city center, much of which was reconstructed during the 1980s with the proceeds of the state's mineral wealth, offers quite a few attractions of its own. There are historic buildings, many parks and gardens, excellent restaurants and some good nightlife venues. But the true delights of this western capital lie a little beyond the city center. Perth is seen at its best at the white sandy beaches of Cottesloe and Scarborough, and on cruises up the Swan River to the vineyards of the fertile Avon Valley. Another Perth highlight is the ferry trip to the atmospheric port town of Fremantle, just 19km downstream.

What to See in Perth

FREMANTLE ✪✪✪

Perth's seaport is reached by train or a short boat trip down the Swan River. Fremantle's harborside location, delightful old buildings and quaint streets make it irresistible. Don't miss the informative Western Australian Maritime Museum, the Fremantle History Museum, the markets, the Round House and the austere Fremantle Prison.

🅿 Fremantle
🚆 Fremantle
ℹ Fremantle Tourist Bureau: Town Hall, Kings Square (☎ (08) 9431 7878)
🕐 Daily 9:30–5

KINGS PARK ✪✪✪

Overlooking the city and the Swan River, this popular 400-hectare reserve consists largely of unspoilt bushland, with colorful wild flowers and prolific birdlife, although it includes the Western Australian Botanic Garden, and the impressive State War Memorial. The best way to explore is by hiring a bike; or join a free guided walking tour.

✉ Off Fraser Avenue
☎ (08) 9480 3600
🕐 Daily 9:30–4
🍴 Restaurants ($–$$)
🚌 33 or Perth Tram bus
♿ Good
🎟 Free

ST GEORGE'S TERRACE ✪✪

A walk along Perth's grandest avenue is the ideal way to see some of the city's historic buildings. Near Pier Street you will find the 1850s Deanery, the Gothic-style St George's Cathedral, and Government House (1864). Closer to Kings Park are the 1850s Old Perth Boys' School, now owned by the National Trust and also containing a gift shop and café, and the Cloisters, an attractive old former collegiate school.

✉ St George's Terrace
🕐 Some buildings open weekdays 9–5.
🚌 City Area Transit bus
♿ Good
🎟 Free
🔁 Kings Park (see above), Western Australian Museum (see below)

An old well at Fremantle's historic Round House

WESTERN AUSTRALIAN MUSEUM ✪✪✪

Incorporating Perth's original 1850s gaol and an early settler's cottage, this is the state's largest and most comprehensive museum. There are displays on Western Australian mammals, birds and marine life, but the highlight is the Aboriginal gallery. While in this northern city area, visit the Art Gallery of Western Australia, on nearby James Street.

✉ Francis Street
☎ (08) 9328 4411
🕐 Mon–Fri & Sun 10:30–5, Sat 1–5. Closed on public holidays
🍴 Coffee shop ($)
🚌 City Area Transit bus
♿ Good
🎟 Free (moderate for special exhibitions)
🔁 St George's Terrace

Did you know ?

Western Australia's capital was originally called the Swan River settlement, after the river which flows through the city. The river itself was named for the black swans which impressed and astonished the 17th-century explorer Willem de Vlamingh and many early settlers. These unusual birds are still common around Perth today.

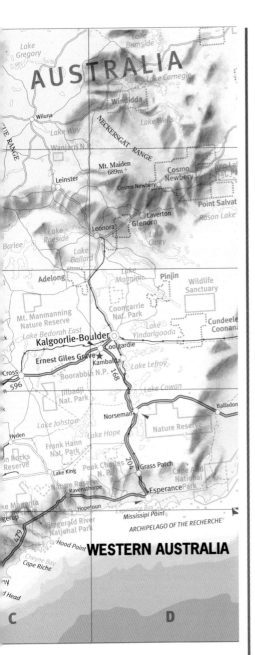

Rugged sandstone gorges are a striking feature of much of Western Australia's ancient landscape

Aptly named Wave Rock

What to See in Western Australia

ALBANY ⚫⚫

Now a scenic holiday resort, Albany was Western Australia's first settlement. Founded three years before Perth, the town developed into a port and whaling center – the old whaling station is now the fascinating Whaleworld museum, and there is whale watching here from August to October. This attractive town contains the 1850s Residency and Old Gaol, both now museums. The coastline and beaches are spectacular, and you should also visit the rugged mountain country of Stirling Range National Park, which lies 70km inland.

➕ 86C1
❌ Albany
↔ Pemberton (see below)
ℹ Albany Tourist Bureau: Old Railway Station, Proudlove Parade
(☎ 1800 644 088
⏱ Mon–Fri 8:15–5:30, Sat–Sun 9–5

KALGOORLIE-BOULDER ⚫⚫

Prospectors flocked to this barren Outback region, 600km east of Perth, when rich gold deposits were discovered near Kalgoorlie in 1893. The area still produces nickel and gold. The modern city of Kalgoorlie and its smaller neighbor, Boulder, contain fine old buildings, the Museum of the Goldfields, the Hannans North Tourist Mine, and a Royal Flying Doctor base. The nearby, well-preserved ghost town of Coolgardie is also worth a visit.

➕ 87D3
❌ Kalgoorlie
ℹ Kalgoorlie-Boulder Tourist Centre: 250 Hannan Street, Kalgoorlie
(☎ (08) 9021 1966)
⏱ Mon–Fri 8:30–5, Sat–Sun 9–5. Closed 25 Dec

THE KIMBERLEY (➤ 22, TOP TEN)

MARGARET RIVER ⚫⚫⚫

Some of Australia's best wines are produced around this picturesque town, 280km south of Perth, in over 50 wineries, including the excellent Vasse Felix and Leeuwin Estate. You can sample the produce at many of them. The area has wonderful beaches, great surfing, and bush-walking along the cliffs of nearby Leeuwin-Naturaliste

➕ 86B1
🚌 Westrail from Perth
ℹ Margaret River Tourist Bureau: Corner Tunbridge Road/Bussell Highway
(☎ (08) 9757 2911) ⏱ Daily 9–5

National Park. The Margaret River township has galleries, crafts shops and fine restaurants.

NAMBUNG NATIONAL ✪✪✪ PARK AND THE PINNACLES

This coastal national park to the north of Perth bristles with thousands of limestone pillars and needles reaching up to 4m in height. Early Dutch seafarers believed they had sighted a ruined city, but the Pinnacles are actually the fossilized remnants of ancient plants. The area has good beaches.

- 86B3
- Nambung National Park, via Cervantes
- (08) 9652 7043
- Daily
- None
- Few
- Cheap

PEMBERTON ✪✪

A visit to the small town of Pemberton, at the heart of the southwest's 'Tall Timber Country', reveals a very different aspect of Western Australia. Giant 400-year-old hardwood trees – jarrah, karri and marri – tower 100m above the dense undergrowth. Ride the Pemberton Tramway through the forests and visit the local sawmill and a museum.

- 86B1
- Westrail from Perth
- Pemberton Tourist Centre: Brockman Street ((08) 9776 1133) Daily 9–5. Closed 25 Dec

ROTTNEST ISLAND ✪✪✪

This idyllic island lies just an hour by ferry or 15 minutes by air from Perth. First discovered by Dutch seafarers in the 17th century and mistakenly named 'rat's nest' for the quokkas (small marsupials that still roam the island today), Rottnest has about 40km of extraordinarily white beaches, crystal-clear waters that are perfect for fishing, diving and snorkeling, and a relaxed, car-free atmosphere.

- 86B1
- Rottnest Island
- Cheap (included in ferry fare)
- Rottnest Island Visitor Centre, Thomson Bay ((08) 9372 9752) Daily 8–5

SHARK BAY MARINE PARK ✪✪

With its islands and 1,500km of indented coastline, the World Heritage area of Shark Bay, on the state's mid-north coast, is a marine wonderland. This vast inlet is famous for the Monkey Mia beach, where wild dolphins come close to the shore to be hand fed. Visit dazzlingly white Shell Beach and François Peron National Park, and see Hamelin Pool's stromatolites, some of the world's oldest living organisms.

- 86A5
- Denham Cheap
- Shark Bay Tourist Centre: 83 Knight Terrace, Denham ((08) 9948 1253) Daily 8–6. Closed 25 Dec

WAVE ROCK ✪✪

This stunning rock formation is one of Western Australia's strangest natural wonders. Wave Rock is a 14m-high granite wall, more than 110m long, which has been eroded over almost 3,000 million years into the shape of a breaking wave. Other curious (and curiously named) formations in the area include the Breakers and the Hippo's Yawn, and you can also look at Aboriginal hand paintings at Mulkas Cave.

- 87C2
- None
- Few Free
- Hyden Tourist Centre: Wave Rock ((08) 9880 5182) Daily

South of Perth

Distance
360km

Time
A full day or more

Start point
Central Perth
🚻 86B2

End point
Central Perth
🚻 86B2

Lunch
Extensions Restaurant ($$)
✉ Bunbury
☎ (08) 9791 2141

*The resort town of
Bunbury offers sandy
beaches, a harbor and the
chance to meet some
wild dolphins*

Taking in beautiful coastal scenery, this drive can just
about be accomplished in a day – or you might want to
stay overnight to fully appreciate the area.

*Leave Perth via the Stirling Highway, then
follow Cockburn Road and Patterson Road to
Rockingham.*

Make a brief stop at Rockingham, an attractive seaside
resort offering excellent beaches and the chance to see
fairy penguins at Penguin Island.

Continue south on the Mandurah Road.

Located on the coast at the mouth of idyllic Peel Inlet,
Mandurah is the perfect spot for swimming, fishing and
boating. There is a local history museum, a bird park, and a
few art and craft galleries.

Continue south on the Old Coast Road.

Yalgorup National Park offers a peaceful environment of
swamps, lakes, dunes and woodland. Birdwatchers should
look out for some of the 100 or so species of waterbird
that frequent the area.

Continue south.

The popular seaside resort of Bunbury
has good beaches and a harbor, and you
might well see dolphins at Koombana
Beach. You can drive further south to see
the tall 400-year-old trees of the Tuart
Forest National Park. If you wish to stay
in the area overnight, continue to
Busselton and Margaret River (➤ 88).

*Head back towards Perth on the
fast South Western Highway.*

On the way back to Perth, stop off at the
historic town of Armadale, 30km from the
city. Highlights are the Pioneer Village – a
re-creation of the early settlement days –
and Cohuna Koala Park, with its varied
collection of Australian wildlife.

Continue on to Perth.

Where To...

Eat and Drink	92–9
Stay	100–3
Shop	104–9
Take Children	110–11
Be Entertained	112–16

Above: *Sandstone gorge on the Murchison River in Kalbarri National Park, Western Australia*
Right: *Look out for koalas!*

New South Wales & Australian Capital Territory

Prices

$	= cheap – under $25
$$	= moderate – $26–$49
$$$	= expensive – over $50

The recommended restaurants on these pages are classified into three price categories. Prices are for a three-course meal for one person, without drinks or service charge.

Eating out in Australia

Although Australia has its share of expensive restaurants, eating out is generally reasonably priced, and you can sample cuisines from all over the world. Restaurants fall into two major types: licensed to serve alcohol, or the popular BYO category – Bring Your Own wine, beer or other liquor. Booking is recommended for most restaurants, and many offer non-smoking areas. There is generally no service charge, and tipping is optional.

New South Wales

Sydney

Bayswater Brasserie ($$)

This stylish brasserie offers Modern Australian food and also has the benefits of a bar and garden seating.

✉ 32 Bayswater Road, Kings Cross ☎ (02) 9357 2177
🕓 Lunch & dinner daily
🚇 Kings Cross

Catalina Rose Bay ($$$)

Right on the harbor, with a fabulous view, outdoor area, and fine seafood.

✉ 1 Sunderland Avenue, Rose Bay ☎ (02) 9371 0555
🕓 Lunch & dinner daily
🚌 324, 325

Doyle's on the Beach ($$–$$$)

Sydney's most famous seafood restaurant, with a wonderful harbor view.

✉ 11 Marine Parade, Watsons Bay ☎ (02) 9337 2007
🕓 Lunch & dinner daily
🚌 324, 325

Hyde Park Barracks Café ($–$$)

Fine Modern Australian food at a good price in the city center. Reserve a courtyard table in advance.

✉ Queens Square, Macquarie Street ☎ (02) 9223 1155
🕓 Mon–Fri 10–4, Sat–Sun 11–3
🚇 Martin Place

Sailors Thai Canteen ($–$$)

One of Sydney's most popular Thai restaurants, this venue offers wonderful food at some very reasonable prices. Book ahead as can get busy.

✉ 106 George Street, The Rocks ☎ (02) 9251 2466
🕓 Lunch & dinner daily
🚇 Circular Quay

Tetsuya's ($$$)

This high-class restaurant blends French, Japanese and Australian food in award-winning combinations. Expensive, but special.

✉ 729 Darling Street, Rozelle ☎ (02) 9555 1017 🕓 Lunch Wed–Sat, dinner Tue–Sat
🚌 440

Blue Mountains

Café Bon Ton ($–$$)

This lively café serves everything from breakfasts to lunch to three-course dinners. There is a large outdoor area, and a log fire burns in winter.

✉ 192 The Mall, Leura ☎ (02) 4782 4377 🕓 All day Wed–Mon. No dinner Tue
🚉 Leura

Darley's ($$$)

Arguably the best restaurant in the Blue Mountains. Fine Modern Australian dining, in a historic building.

✉ Lilianfels Blue Mountains, Lilianfels Avenue, Katoomba ☎ (02) 4780 1200 🕓 Lunch & dinner Wed–Sun 🚉 Katoomba

Byron Bay

The Orient Café Restaurant ($$)

Excellent Modern Australian meals in an elegant, old-world environment. A veranda table is recommended (early reservation a good idea).

✉ Main Roundabout, Jonson Street ☎ (02) 6685 7771
🕓 Lunch & dinner daily
🚉 None

Coffs Harbour

Avanti ($$)

This popular Italian restaurant serves fine home-made pastas, and traditional meat dishes.

✉ 368 High Street ☎ (02) 6652 4818 🕓 Closed Sun 🚉 None

Hunter Valley
Robert's at Pepper Tree ($$$)
Specializing in country-style food, this delightfully atmospheric establishment is surrounded by Hunter Valley grapevines.

✉ **Halls Road, Pokolbin** ☎ **(02) 4998 7330** 🕐 Lunch & dinner daily 🚌 None

Kiama
Duart's ($$)
Good Modern Australian food is served in and on the veranda of a historic building.

✉ **127 Terralong Street** ☎ **(02) 4233 1758** 🕐 Lunch & dinner daily 🚌 None

Lord Howe Island
Williams ($$)
One of the best on Lord Howe, this restaurant offers fine, innovative food in a bright, breezy environment.

✉ **Trader Nick's, Old Settlement Beach** ☎ **(02) 6563 2002** 🕐 Dinner daily 🚌 None

Southern Highlands
The Grand Bar and Brasserie ($$)
A bright city-style brasserie that offers a changing Modern Australian menu. Plenty to choose from; enjoy the fun atmosphere.

✉ **The Grand Arcade, 295 Bong Bong Street, Bowral** ☎ **(02) 4861 4783** 🕐 Lunch & dinner daily 🚌 Bowral

Janeks Café ($)
Small, lively café, offering good value, from breakfasts through lunch to three-course dinners.

✉ **Corbett Plaza, Wingecarribee Street, Bowral** ☎ **(02) 4861 4414** 🕐 Lunch Mon–Sat, dinner Thu–Sat 🚌 Bowral

Canberra & the Australian Capital Territory

Canberra City
Café Barocca ($–$$)
One of central Canberra's most popular cafés, with a bar, outdoor dining and an interesting Modern Australian menu. Something for everyone at reasonable prices.

✉ **60 Marcus Clarke Street, Canberra City** ☎ **(02) 6248 0253** 🕐 Lunch & dinner Mon–Fri, 🚌 301

Gus's Coffee Lounge ($)
This tiny Canberra institution is a great, cheap place for excellent coffee, snacks, and main meals like pasta and seafood.

✉ **Corner Bunda Street and Garema Place, Canberra City** ☎ **(02) 6248 8118** 🕐 Daily 7:30AM–late 🚌 301

The Oak Room ($$$)
Within the city's best hotel, the Hyatt, this centrally located restaurant has a fine reputation both for its professional service and its inventive Modern Australian fare.

✉ **Hyatt Hotel Canberra, Commonwealth Avenue, Yarralumla** ☎ **(02) 6270 8977** 🕐 Lunch Tue–Fri, dinner Tue–Sat 🚌 231, 267

Ottoman Cuisine ($$)
This highly acclaimed Turkish restaurant offers something different. Specializing in seafood, it is one of Canberra's hottest dining spots.

✉ **8 Franklin Street (upstairs), Manuka** ☎ **(02) 6239 6754** 🕐 Lunch Mon–Fri, dinner Mon–Sat 🚌 238, 310

Modern Australian Cuisine
Acclaimed by 'foodies' the world over, Modern Australian cuisine has its roots in the nation's multiculturalism. By using the freshest produce and combining cuisines as varied as Thai and Mediterranean, Australian chefs are creating taste sensations in every major city. 'Bush tucker' – consisting of ingredients generally considered traditional Aboriginal fare – is also popular, and you can sample unusual delicacies like crocodile, kangaroo, possum and emu.

Queensland

Australian Seafood
With an extraordinary range of produce from the sea, it is not surprising that Australia boasts so many excellent seafood restaurants. Every major city offers at least a couple of really good places that serve this cuisine, and many coastal towns have their own specialities. Tuna from South Australia, Tasmania's Atlantic salmon, Sydney rock oysters, Brisbane's Moreton Bay bugs, and the tropical fish, barramundi, are all highly recommended.

Brisbane
About Face ($$–$$$)
Located in a historic coach house, this wonderful restaurant offers an acclaimed modern French menu.
✉ 252 Kelvin Grove Road, Kelvin Grove ☎ (07) 3356 8605 🕐 Lunch Fri, dinner daily 🚌 172, 504

Baguette ($$–$$$)
A long-running restaurant with a fine reputation and a menu that exhibits French, Australian and Asian influences.
✉ 150 Racecourse Road, Ascot ☎ (07) 3268 6168 🕐 Lunch & dinner daily 🚌 160, 180

City Gardens Café ($–$$)
Set in Brisbane's lush Botanic Gardens, this delightful café serves coffees and delicious meals and snacks.
✉ Botanic Gardens, Alice Street ☎ (07) 3229 1554 🕐 Breakfast, lunch & afternoon tea daily 🚌 City Circle 333

Lucky's Trattoria ($–$$)
Excellent Italian cooking with a varied menu featuring home-made pastas. There are lots of good restaurants in this area.
✉ 683 Ann St, Fortitude Valley ☎ (07) 3252 2353; 🕐 Dinner Mon–Sun 🚌 191, 232

The Malaysian Experience ($$)
A reliable Malaysian restaurant with some particularly good noodle and laksa dishes.
✉ 80 Jephson Street, Toowong ☎ (07) 3870 2646 🕐 Lunch Mon–Sat, dinner daily 🚌 Toowong

Michael's Riverside Restaurant ($$$)
In a prime riverfront position with wonderful views, this popular restaurant offers Mediterranean and international cuisine.
✉ Riverside Centre, 123 Eagle Street ☎ (07) 3832 5522 🕐 Lunch Sun–Fri, dinner Mon–Sat 🚌 City Circle 333

Pier Nine Oyster Bar and Seafood Grill ($$$)
A great central centre venue for sampling excellent oysters, lobster and other seafood. Despite its name, the restaurant also serves meat dishes.
✉ Eagle Street Pier, 1 Eagle Street ☎ (07) 3229 2194 🕐 Lunch & dinner daily 🚌 City Circle 333

Tropical North Queensland
Catalina Restaurant ($$)
With its French and Asian cuisine and delightful veranda seating, this Port Douglas eatery is a winner.
✉ 22 Wharf Street, Port Douglas ☎ (07) 4099 5287 🕐 Dinner Tue–Sun 🚌 None

Fishlips Bar and Grill ($$)
A wonderful seafood menu, including local barramundi. This is one of the best places to eat in Cairns.
✉ 228 Sheridan Street, Cairns ☎ (07) 4041 1700 🕐 Lunch Fri, dinner daily 🚌 None

Perrotta's at the Gallery ($)
This art gallery eatery has a varied and interesting menu and, as a bonus, there are great views of the ocean from its outside seating. The low prices too are an added attraction.

✉ **Regional Art Gallery, Corner Abbott and Shields Streets, Cairns** ☎ (07) 4031 5899
🕐 Lunch & dinner daily
🚭 None

Nautilus ($$$)

Fine seafood is the speciality of this glamorous tropical restaurant, set in a rainforest environment.
✉ **17 Murphy Street, Port Douglas** ☎ (07) 4099 5330
🕐 Dinner daily 🚭 None

Red Ochre Grill ($$)

You can sample a variety of unusual Aussie bush tucker here, from a menu that includes crocodile and almost 40 other native foodstuffs.
✉ **43 Shields Street, Cairns**
☎ (07) 4051 0100 🕐 Lunch Mon–Sat, dinner daily
🚭 None

Gold Coast

Imperial Plaza ($$–$$$)

Take your pick from three great restaurants: Times Cafe (steak, seafood, pasta); Mikado (Japanese); Imperial Palace (Chinese).
✉ **cnr Elkhorn Ave & Gold Coast Highway, Surfers Paradise**
☎ (07) 5538 3211/5538 2788/5538 5944 🕐 Open 7 days
🚭 1, 1A

Kairo Cafe ($$)

A blend of Asian and Mediterranean cuisines makes this café a fun eatery. Live weekend performances.
✉ **The Phoenician, cnr Surf Pde & Queensland Av, Broadbeach** ☎ (07) 5531 5868
🕐 Lunch & dinner daily
🚭 1, 1A

Metro on Main ($$)

With an outdoor dining area and a varied Modern Australian menu, this is a good spot for lunch or dinner. The restaurant is at the heart of the Gold Coast's main dining area.
✉ **2/20 Tedder Avenue, Main Beach** ☎ (07) 5528 0281
🕐 Lunch Thu–Sun, dinner daily 🚭 1, 1A

Sunshine Coast

Chilli Jam Café ($–$$)

A particularly good Thai restaurant with delightful decor, only a short drive from the main town of Noosa Heads.
✉ **195 Weyba Road, Noosaville** ☎ (07) 5449 9755
🕐 Dinner Tue–Sun 🚭 None

Lindoni's Ristorante ($$)

With its fine traditional food and wines, this is the Sunshine Coast's best Italian restaurant.
✉ **Hastings Street, Noosa Heads** ☎ (07) 5447 5111
🕐 Dinner daily 🚭 None

Saltwater ($$)

The fresh seafood here includes wonderful fish and chips, and some rather more innovative dishes. There is a bar, and the restaurant offers outdoor eating.
✉ **8 Hastings Street, Noosa Heads** ☎ (07) 5447 2234
🕐 Lunch & dinner daily
🚭 None

Artis ($$)

This award-winning restaurant serves excellent French and European-Australian dishes in an unusual Alpine-style A-frame building.
✉ **8 Noosa Drive, Noosa Heads** ☎ (07) 5447 2300
🕐 Lunch Wed–Sun, dinner Tue–Sun 🚭 None

Asian Cuisines

Australia's proximity to Asia, and the fact that the country has a substantial Asian population, have led to oriental food becoming extremely popular. Generally, Indian restaurants are not as good as in many other parts of the world, but there are plenty of high-quality Thai, Indonesian, Malaysian, Korean, Japanese, Vietnamese, Chinese and other Asian eateries in which to enjoy these exotic cuisines.

Victoria & Tasmania

Melbourne's Restaurants

Although Sydney would dispute the claim, Melbourne likes to regard itself as Australia's culinary capital. There are some 4,000 restaurants, and dining out is a favourite Melbourne pastime. With 170 or so ethnic groups among the city's population, the variety of cuisines is extraordinary – everything from Spanish to Korean is represented – and there are prices to suit every budget.

Victoria

Melbourne

Café Di Stasio ($$–$$$)
Popular Italian restaurant serving hand-made pasta and fine meat and seafood dishes.
✉ 31 Fitzroy Street, St Kilda
☎ (03) 9525 3999
🕐 Lunch & dinner daily
🚋 Any St Kilda tram

Flower Drum ($$$)
This high-quality Chinese restaurant offers an unusual menu that has received many accolades.
✉ 17 Market Lane
☎ (03) 9662 3655
🕐 Lunch Mon–Sat, dinner daily 🚋 City Circle tram

Il Solito Posto ($–$$)
Excellent Italian fare on two levels – a downstairs dining room, and a cheaper bistro.
✉ Shop 4, 113 Collins Street
☎ (03) 9654 4466
🕐 Lunch & dinner Mon–Sat
🚋 City Circle tram

Langton's Restaurant and Wine Bar ($$$)
High quality seasonally-based French cuisine in plush surrounds.
✉ 69 Flinders Lane, Melbourne
☎ (03) 9663 0222 🕐 Lunch Mon–Fri, dinner Mon–Sat
🚋 City Circle tram

Donovans ($$–$$$)
In a wonderful position on St Kilda's seafront, Donovans serves superb seafood in elegant surroundings.
✉ 40 Jacka Boulevard, St Kilda ☎ (03) 9534 8221
🕐 Lunch & dinner daily
🚋 Any St Kilda tram

Stella ($$–$$$)
One of Melbourne's favorite Modern Australian

restaurants. Innovative food and stylish décor.
✉ 159 Spring Street
☎ (03) 9639 1555
🕐 Lunch Mon–Fri, dinner daily
🚋 City Circle tram

Ballarat

Ansonia ($$)
Excellent modern Australian fare in a smart boutique hotel.
✉ 32 Lydiard Street South
☎ (03) 5332 4678
🕐 Breakfast, lunch & dinner daily 🚋 Ballarat

Rutherglen

All Saints Winery ($$)
A Modern Australian menu, using the best local produce, in a popular hills café.
✉ All Saints Road, Wahgunyah ☎ (02) 6033 1922
🕐 Lunch daily 🚋 None

Great Ocean Road

Chris's Beacon Point Restaurant ($$–$$$)
This restaurant serves innovative seafood and Greek-influenced meals, and has a superb ocean view.
✉ Skenes Creek Road, Skenes Creek, near Apollo Bay
☎ (03) 5237 6411 🕐 Lunch & dinner daily 🚋 None

Pisces on the Park ($$)
Local seafood and a spectacular sea view are the specialities of this pleasant eatery.
✉ Great Ocean Road, Apollo Bay ☎ (03) 5237 7118
🕐 Dinner Tue–Sun 🚋 None

Phillip Island

The Jetty ($$)
Phillip Island's premier restaurant offers fine local lobster and other seafood.
✉ The Esplanade, Cowes
☎ (03) 5952 2060 🕐 Lunch & dinner daily 🚋 None

Tasmania

Hobart
Blue Skies Dining ($$)
This large and lively brasserie, right on the waterfront, has a great atmosphere to accompany its innovative Modern Australian cuisine.
✉ Ground Floor, Murray Street Pier ☎ (03) 6224 3747
🕐 Lunch & dinner daily
🚭 None

Mit Zitrone ($$–$$$)
Awarded Remy Martin Best Tasmanian Restaurant for its delicious Cape-style modern Australian cuisine.
✉ 333 Elizabeth Street, Hobart
☎ (03) 6234 8113
🕐 Lunch and dinner Tue–Sat
🚭 None

The Drunken Admiral ($$)
In a historic waterfront building, this lively eatery specializes in fine seafood. Enjoy the surroundings as much as the food.
✉ 17–19 Hunter Street
☎ (03) 6234 1903
🕐 Dinner daily 🚭 None

Mures Upper Deck ($$–$$$)
Hobart's best known restaurant offers a wonderful range of seafood, a lively atmosphere, and good waterfront views.
✉ Mures Fish Centre, Victoria Dock
☎ (03) 6231 1999
🕐 Lunch & dinner daily
🚭 None

Retro Café ($)
A very popular daytime-only café that serves good coffee, hearty breakfasts and wholesome lunches. Great value refuelling.

✉ Corner Salamanca Place and Montpelier Retreat
☎ (03) 6223 3073
🕐 Breakfast & lunch daily
🚭 None

Devonport
The Old Rectory ($$)
Devonport's classiest restaurant offers a fine seasonal à la carte menu.
✉ 71 Wright Street
☎ (03) 6427 8037
🕐 Dinner Mon–Sat 🚭 None

Launceston
Fee and Me ($$–$$$)
One of Tasmania's best Modern Australian restaurants.
✉ 190 Charles Street
☎ (03) 6331 3195
🕐 Dinner Mon–Sat
🚭 None

Star Bar Café ($–$$)
The ideal place for a snack, coffee and cake, or a good-value main meal. There is also a bar.
✉ 113 Charles Street
☎ (03) 6331 9659
🕐 Lunch & dinner daily
🚭 None

Port Arthur
Eaglehawk ($$)
Dine on freshly caught seafood in an old shipwright's house.
✉ Arthur Highway, Eaglehawk Neck ☎ (03) 6250 3331
🕐 Lunch & dinner daily
🚭 None

Strahan
Franklin Manor ($$–$$$)
A surprisingly upmarket restaurant for this small west-coast town, with food described as 'casual modern'.
✉ The Esplanade
☎ (03) 6471 7311
🕐 Dinner daily 🚭 None

Tasmanian Produce
Among Australia's array of fresh, flavorsome produce that has had such a strong influence on the new 'Modern Oz' cuisine, Tasmania's home-grown products stand out. There is wonderful seafood such as Atlantic salmon, ocean trout and crayfish; superb Bries, Camemberts and other gourmet cheeses; fine meats; and fruit and vegetables with real taste. To wash it all down, Tasmania's excellent wines are some of Australia's finest.

South Australia & Northern Territory

'Tourist Restaurants'
Australia's major cities all have an array of dining options particularly designed for tourists. Many such restaurants are in scenic locations, and though the standard of cuisine is not always out of the ordinary, it's worth sampling a few. You can dine while cruising Sydney Harbour or the Brisbane River, or at the top of tall buildings with spectacular views; and you can sample Aussie 'bush tucker' in most capital cities.

South Australia

Adelaide
Blake's ($$$)
An elegant, central hotel restaurant with an innovative Modern Australian menu. Good service.
✉ **Hyatt Regency Hotel, North Terrace**
☎ **(08) 8238 2381**
🕐 **Lunch Thu–Fri, dinner Mon–Sat** 🚌 **99B, City Loop**

Charlick's Feed Store ($$$)
This elegant restaurant offers Modern Australian cuisine and is run by Adelaide's top foodies including Maggie Beer.
✉ **Ebenezer Place, City**
☎ **(08) 8223 7566** 🕐 **Lunch & dinner daily except Sat**
🚌 **City Loop**

Universal Wine Bar ($$)
With its great atmosphere and imaginative cuisine, this is one of Adelaide's favorites. Book ahead to ensure a table.
✉ **285 Rundle Street**
☎ **(08) 8232 5000** 🕐 **Lunch & dinner Mon–Sat** 🚌 **City Loop**

Adelaide Hills
Bridgewater Mill ($$$)
One of Australia's best. Modern Australian cuisine in a historic gold flour mill.
✉ **Mount Barker Road, Bridgewater** ☎ **(08) 8339 3422**
🕐 **Lunch Thur–Mon** 🚌 **None**

Barossa Valley
1918 Bistro and Grill ($$)
Delicious country-style food is the speciality of this rustic restaurant in the heart of the Barossa Valley.
✉ **94 Murray Street, Tanunda**
☎ **(08) 8563 0405**
🕐 **Lunch & dinner daily**
🚌 **None**

Kangaroo Island
Ozone Seafront Hotel ($$$)
A family bistro with a wide variety of food served from breakfast to dinner.
✉ **The Foreshore, Kingscote**
☎ **(08) 8553 2011**
🕐 **Breakfast, lunch & dinner daily** 🚌 **None**

Northern Territory

Darwin
Christo's on the Wharf ($$–$$$)
There are wonderful Darwin water views from this popular seafood restaurant, with its large outdoor dining area. Reservations are recommended.
✉ **Stokes Hill Wharf**
☎ **(08) 8981 8658**
🕐 **Lunch Tue–Fri, dinner daily**
🚌 **None**

The Hanuman ($$)
Acclaimed Thai and Nonya (Malaysian) cuisine in an elegant setting.
✉ **28 Mitchell Street**
☎ **(08) 8941 3500**
🕐 **Lunch Mon–Fri, dinner daily**
🚌 **None**

Alice Springs
Ristorante Puccini ($$)
One of the Alice's best eateries: family-owned and serving above-average Italian food. Nice atmosphere and friendly service.
✉ **Ansett Building, Todd Mall**
☎ **(08) 8953 0935**
🕐 **Lunch Thu–Fri, dinner daily**
🚌 **None**

Uluru
Most of the Ayers Rock Resort restaurants, bars and cafés are within the main hotels – such as the very good Sails in the Desert (➤ 103).

Western Australia

Western Australia

Perth

Bellissimo ($–$$)

The menu at this popular suburban Italian eatery includes fine pastas and wood-oven baked pizzas.

✉ 3 Bay View Terrace, Claremont ☎ (08) 9385 3588 🕐 Lunch Tue–Sat, dinner daily 🚌 City Area Transit bus

Fraser's ($$)

Top city and river views, good service and an imaginative Modern Australian menu are on offer here.

✉ Fraser Avenue, Kings Park, West Perth ☎ (08) 9481 7100 🕐 Breakfast, lunch & dinner daily 🚌 33

The Garden Restaurant ($$$)

The perfect venue for a special night out. The Garden offers classically influenced food and fine wines.

✉ Parmelia Hilton, Mill Street ☎ (08) 9322 3622 🕐 Dinner Tue–Sat 🚌 City Area Transit bus

The Loose Box ($$$)

Although a half-hour drive from the city, this is arguably Western Australia's best restaurant. The cuisine is classical French, and this award-winning venue has overnight accommodation in luxury chalets.

✉ 6825 Great Eastern Highway, Mundaring ☎ (08) 9295 1787 🕐 Lunch Fri & Sun, dinner Wed–Sat 🚌 None

Albany

Kookas ($$)

An old colonial house which has been converted into a charming restaurant serving fine country food.

✉ 204 Stirling Terrace ☎ (08) 9841 5889 🕐 Lunch Tue–Fri, dinner Tue–Sat 🚌 None

Bunbury

Louisa's ($$–$$$)

This delightful restaurant in an old colonial house offers a Modern Australian menu.

✉ 15 Clifton Street ☎ (08) 9721 9959 🕐 Dinner Tue–Sat 🚌 None

Fremantle

Chunagon ($$$)

A renowned Japanese restaurant with fine views of the harbor and the ocean.

✉ 46 Mews Road ☎ (08) 9336 1000 🕐 Lunch & dinner daily 🚌 Fremantle

Quattro ($$)

This lively, open-all-hours café/brasserie offers modern Italian-style food, and has become a favorite Fremantle eating place. The antipasti and crisp pizzas are particularly good.

✉ 26 Marine Terrace ☎ (08) 9336 4500 🕐 24 hours daily 🚌 Fremantle

Kalgoorlie-Boulder

Basil's on Hannan ($$)

Kalgoorlie is not known for its cuisine, but this central café offers good-value meals in pleasant surroundings.

✉ 168 Hannan Street, Kalgoorlie ☎ (08) 9021 7832 🕐 Lunch daily, dinner Mon–Sat 🚌 None

Margaret River

Leeuwin Estate ($$)

With an emphasis on fresh local produce, this elegant but casual winery restaurant offers excellent service and Modern Australian dishes.

✉ Stevens Road ☎ (08) 9757 6253 🕐 Lunch daily, dinner Sat 🚌 None

The Café Scene

Australia's thriving café scene provides plenty of options for inexpensive dining. Every capital city, and many of the larger towns, have lively cafés that serve snacks and light meals for $10 or less. Many of these eateries have outdoor dining areas – often as simple as a few pavement tables – which are wonderful for the warmer months, and you will generally find excellent coffee to accompany your meal.

New South Wales & Canberra

Prices

$	= under $100
$$	= $100 – $240
$$$	= over $250

The recommended hotels on these pages are classified into three price categories. Prices are per room per night, regardless of single or double occupancy.

Accommodation in Australia

Australia offers a wide variety of accommodation. There are world-class city hotels like Sydney's Park Hyatt, and luxurious island resorts such as Queensland's Hayman Island. You can stay on working farms to experience country and Outback life, or book into a historic Tasmanian cottage for bed and breakfast. Cheaper options are motels and Aussie hotels – functional yet often atmospheric pubs.

New South Wales

Sydney
Park Hyatt Sydney ($$$)
One of Sydney's very best hotels, with a fabulous site opposite the Opera House.
✉ **7 Hickson Road, The Rocks**
☎ **(02) 9241 1234** 🚍 **431–434**

The Russell ($$)
This small Victorian hotel has individually styled rooms, a roof garden and is close to the Rocks and city center.
✉ **143a George Street, The Rocks** ☎ **(02) 9241 3543**
🚊 **Circular Quay**

Manhattan Hotel ($$)
The renovated art deco-style Manhattan represents very good value. It is also within easy reach of the city.
✉ **8 Greenknowe Avenue, Elizabeth Bay** ☎ **(02) 9358 1288**
🚊 **Kings Cross**

Blue Mountains
Mountain Heritage Country House Retreat ($$–$$$)
This historic hotel offers an ideal location, superb views and a range of good-value accommodation.
✉ **Corner Apex and Lovel Streets, Katoomba**
☎ **(02) 4782 2155**
🚊 **Katoomba**

Coffs Harbour
Aanuka Beach Resort ($$$)
Set on a white sandy beach, this attractive hotel offers suites furnished with antiques, and delightful gardens
✉ **Firman Drive, Diggers Beach** ☎ **(02) 6652 7555**
🚊 **Coffs Harbour**

Hunter Valley
The Convent Pepper Tree ($$$)
One of the Hunter Valley's best hotels, the historic Convent provides attractive, spacious rooms that open onto a veranda. There is an outdoor pool and tennis courts.
✉ **Halls Road, Pokolbin**
☎ **(02) 4998 7764** 🚍 **Pokolbin**

Lord Howe Island
Somerset ($$)
This large self-catering lodge provides pleasant units that all include a private veranda. This makes for a relaxing venue for a visit: the rooms are well equipped, and the pleasant tropical gardens contain several barbecue areas.
✉ **Neds Beach Road**
☎ **(02) 6563 2061** 🚍 **None**

Canberra
Hyatt Hotel Canberra ($$$)
This is indisputably the national capital's finest (also expensive) hotel, in a great location close to most of the city's main attractions. The renovated 1920s building is charming, the rooms are spacious, and there are extensive, well-maintained gardens in which to relax.
✉ **Commonwealth Avenue, Yarralumla** ☎ **(02) 6270 1234**
🚍 **231, 267**

Olims Canberra Hotel ($$)
This good-value hotel is based around an attractive heritage listed building. Rooms and suites are available, and there are two restaurants plus a bar.
✉ **Corner Ainslie and Limestone Avenues, Braddon**
☎ **(02) 6248 5511; fax (02) 6247 0864** 🚍 **302, 362**

Queensland & Victoria

Queensland

Brisbane
The Heritage ($$$)
This luxurious hotel has a fine location: on the waterfront and close to the Botanic Gardens.
✉ **Corner Edward and Margaret Streets** ☎ **(07) 3221 1999** 🚋 **City Circle 333**

Gazebo Hotel Brisbane ($$)
Modern comforts in a quiet, pleasant setting. This popular establishment is a short walk from the city center.
✉ **345 Wickham Terrace**
☎ **(07) 3831 6177**
🚋 **City Circle 333**

Cairns
The Reef Hotel Casino ($$$)
Part of the glossy Cairns casino complex, this hotel provides all the expected luxuries and a few more besides.
✉ **35–41 Wharf Street**
☎ **(07) 4030 8888** 🚋 **None**

Gold Coast
Diamonds Resort ($–$$)
As an alternative to the expensive Gold Coast hotels, this central Surfers Paradise resort has apartments as well as cheaper motel-style rooms.
✉ **19 Orchid Avenue, Surfers Paradise** ☎ **(07) 5570 1011**
🚋 **1, 1A**

Sunshine Coast
Netanya Noosa ($$–$$$)
This delightful low-rise resort, right on the beachfront, offers luxury and relaxation at an affordable price.
✉ **75 Hastings Street, Noosa Heads**
☎ **(07) 5447 4722** 🚋 **None**

Victoria

Melbourne
Holiday Inn on Flinders ($$–$$$)
This modern, stylish hotel offers a variety of room types. It has a bar, a popular brasserie, a sauna and heated swimming pool.
✉ **Corner Flinders Lane & Spencer Street**
☎ **(03) 9629 4111**
🚋 **City Circle tram**

The Victoria Hotel ($–$$)
In a convenient location behind the Town Hall, the historic Victoria offers extremely good value.
✉ **215 Little Collins Street**
☎ **(03) 9653 0441**
🚋 **Any Swanston Walk tram**

The Windsor ($$$)
This 1883 National Trust hotel provides both Victorian elegance and charm plus good service and facilities in a city center location.
✉ **103 Spring Street** ☎ **(03) 9633 6000** 🚋 **City Circle tram**

Great Ocean Road
The Cumberland Lorne ($$$)
An award-winning apartment-style resort; the ideal base for exploring the Great Ocean Road.
✉ **150 Mountjoy Parade, Lorne**
☎ **(03) 5289 2400** 🚋 **None**

Phillip Island
Kaloha Holiday Resort ($$)
In Phillip Island's main town of Cowes, this resort offers fully self-contained, one- and two-bedroom units at moderate rates.
✉ **Corner of Steele & Chapel Streets, Cowes**
☎ **(03) 5952 2179**

Queensland's Island Resorts
In addition to the Queensland accommodations detailed here, there are many island resorts close to, or even on, the Great Barrier Reef. From the sophisticated luxury of Lizard Island to the family-oriented resorts on islands like South Molle in the Whitsunday region, there is something for every taste and budget. You can also stay right on the reef – Heron and Lady Elliot islands are the best bets.

Tasmania & South Australia

Serviced Apartments
Serviced apartments are
a very popular
accommodation option.
These self-catering units
have from one to three
bedrooms, and generally
have a separate
lounge/kitchen area.
Such apartments are
usually cheaper than
hotels of a comparable
standard, and are ideal
for families, small
groups, or those who
just want the freedom to
cook 'at home'.

Tasmania

Hobart

Islington Private Hotel ($$)
There are just eight
delightfully furnished rooms
in this converted 1845
mansion. The hotel is just
outside the city center.
⊠ 321 Davey Street
☎ (03) 6223 3900 🚌 None

Lenna of Hobart ($$)
This good mid-priced motel
has an elegant restaurant
housed in an 1870s mansion.
⊠ 20 Runnymede Street,
Battery Point
☎ (03) 6232 3900 🚌 None

Freycinet Peninsula

Freycinet Lodge ($$–$$$)
Set in Freycinet National
Park, this timber lodge offers
high-quality accommodation
and total tranquillity. Guests
stay in one- or two-bedroom,
comfortably furnished cabins
that feature a private balcony.
The lodge also has a tennis
court and licensed restaurant.
⊠ Freycinet National Park,
Coles Bay
☎ (03) 6257 0101 🚌 None

Launceston

Old Bakery Inn ($$)
A beautifully restored inn
with a selection of
accommodation types –
guests can choose between
converted stables, a cottage,
or the old bakery itself.
⊠ 270 York Street
☎ (03) 6331 7900 🚌 None

Strahan

Franklin Manor ($$$)
Once a private home, this
small, welcoming hotel is the
pick of the West Coast
accommodation.
⊠ The Esplanade
☎ (03) 6471 7311 🚌 None

South Australia

Adelaide

**Hyatt Regency Adelaide
($$$)**
Adelaide's best hotel, right in
the heart of the city, provides
the ultimate in luxury.
⊠ North Terrace
☎ (08) 8231 1234;
fax (08) 8231 1120
🚌 City Loop or 99B

Earl of Zetland Hotel ($)
This popular city-center pub
offers comfortable rooms at
bargain prices.
⊠ 44 Flinders Street
☎ (08) 8223 5500
🚌 City Loop

Barossa Valley

**The Hermitage of
Marananga ($$–$$$)**
On a hill overlooking the
vineyards, this hotel is
spacious, with a pleasant
ambience.
⊠ Corner Seppeltsfield and
Stonewell Roads, Marananga
☎ (08) 8562 2722; fax (08) 8562
3133 🚌 None

Flinders Ranges

**Wilpena Pound Resort
($–$$)**
In the heart of the ranges,
this resort provides motel-
style rooms, caravans and
powered campsites.
⊠ Wilpena Pound
☎ (08) 8648 0004.
Adelaide office: (08) 8415 5555
🚌 None

Kangaroo Island

Ozone Seafront Hotel ($–$$)
Set on the seafront, the
Ozone provides some of the
island's best accommodation
at reasonable prices.
⊠ The Esplanade, Kingscote
☎ (08) 8553 2011
🚌 None

Northern Territory & Western Australia

Northern Territory

Darwin

The Carlton Darwin ($$$)
One of Darwin's best hotels, in a modern, pastel-colored building. Offers a variety of room types – from standard to executive suites – and excellent facilities, including a restaurant, gymnasium and swimming pool.
✉ The Esplanade
☎ (08) 8980 0800; fax (08) 8980 0888 🚌 None

Hotel Darwin ($$)
This old colonial-style hotel is full of atmosphere, and it provides accommodation at very reasonable rates.
✉ 10 Herbert Street
☎ (08) 8981 9211 🚌 None

Alice Springs

Alice Springs Resort ($$–$$$)
This pleasant resort hotel offers a variety of accommodation, from family rooms to a more luxurious standard.
✉ 34 Stott Terrace
☎ (08) 8952 6699 🚌 None

Katherine

Frontier Katherine ($–$$)
In addition to its comfortable motel-style rooms, the Frontier offers budget caravans.
✉ Stuart Highway
☎ (08) 8972 1744; fax (08) 8972 2790 🚌 None

Uluru

Sails in the Desert ($$$)
With its distinctive architecture and excellent facilities, this is the best place to stay in the Uluru area.
✉ Yulara Drive, Ayers Rock Resort
☎ (08) 8956 2200 🚌 None

Western Australia

Perth

Hyatt Regency Perth ($$$)
Located beside the Swan River, this luxurious hotel is one of the best in Perth.
✉ 99 Adelaide Terrace
☎ (08) 9225 1234
🚌 City Area Transit bus

Miss Maud Swedish Hotel ($$)
This long-time Perth favorite is centrally located and provides old-style charm and excellent value.
✉ 97 Murray Street
☎ (08) 9325 3900; fax (08) 9221 3225
🚌 City Area Transit bus

Kalgoorlie–Boulder

York Hotel ($–$$)
Dating from the early 1900s, this atmospheric hotel has stained-glass windows to add to its charm.
✉ 259 Hannan Street, Kalgoorlie
☎ (08) 9021 2337
🚌 None

The Kimberley

El Questro Station ($–$$$)
This vast cattle station provides everything from campsites and bungalows to luxurious rooms in the exclusive Homestead.
✉ Gibb River Road, via Kununurra
☎ (08) 9169 1777
❌ El Questro Station

Margaret River

Cape Lodge ($$$)
An award-winning lodge with colonial furniture, light airy rooms and a relaxed rural atmosphere.
✉ Caves Road, Yallingup
☎ fax (08) 9755 6311
🚌 None

Wilderness Accommodation
Many of the continent's most scenic regions – national parks like Kakadu and the Flinders Ranges, the World Heritage areas of the Tasmanian wilderness and some of the Great Barrier Reef islands – have little in the way of hotel accommodation. You can, however, camp for a small fee in many of these parks and reserves, while others provide basic but cosy cabins and huts.

Australiana

Opening Times

Australian shops offer an excellent range of goods and relatively competitive prices – Sydney and Melbourne in particular have a wide variety of retail outlets, selling everything from designer clothing to high-quality souvenirs. Shopping hours are generally 9–5:30 on weekdays and 9–5 on Saturdays. Many large stores and suburban shopping centers are also open on Sundays, and each capital city offers late shopping on one night.

New South Wales
Done Art & Design
Ken Done's incredibly popular and colorful designs are found on beachwear, T-shirts, accessories and homewares.
- ✉ 123 George Street, The Rocks, Sydney
- ☎ (02) 9251 6099
- 🚇 Circular Quay

Dorian Scott
In addition to Akubra hats and other Aussie bush and country clothing, this excellent shop sells colorful hand-knits and Australian-designed clothing.
- ✉ 105 George Street, The Rocks, Sydney
- ☎ (02) 9221 8145
- 🚇 Circular Quay

R M Williams
This is the original 'Bushman's Outfitters', where you can buy Akubra hats, Drizabone oilskin coats and durable country-style clothing.
- ✉ 389 George Street, Sydney
- ☎ (02) 9262 2228
- 🚇 Town Hall

Australian Capital Territory
Australian Choice
This shop sells only good Australian-made products, and is great for gifts and souvenirs.
- ✉ Canberra Center, Bunda Street, Canberra City
- ☎ (02) 6257 5315
- 🚌 301

Queensland
Australian Woolshed
This major attraction (► 110) includes the excellent Supply Store, which offers high-quality Australian gifts and souvenirs.

- ✉ 148 Samford Road, Ferny Hills, Brisbane
- ☎ (07) 3351 5366
- 🚉 Ferny Grove

Victoria
Chapel Street
Australian designer fashions are well represented on this lively street which stretches through a couple of inner city suburbs.
- ✉ South Yarra and Prahran, Melbourne 🚊 Trams 6, 8, 72

Coogi Connections
This shop specializes in Australia's colorful Coogi 'artistry knitwear', which uses unique colors, patterns and designs.
- ✉ 86 Collins Street, Melbourne
- ☎ (03) 9650 4407
- 🚊 City Circle tram

Tasmania
The Tasmania Shop
Tasmania's wonderful produce, including honey and other foodstuffs, woolen clothing and craftworks are sold in this specialty outlet.
- ✉ 108 Elizabeth Street, Hobart
- ☎ (03) 6231 5200 🚌 None

South Australia
South Australian Museum
This museum shop is a good place to find some unusual Australian gifts and souvenirs.
- ✉ North Terrace, Adelaide
- ☎ (08) 8207 7500
- 🚌 City Loop or 99B

Western Australia
London Court
This mock-Tudor style arcade – a tourist attraction in itself – offers a wide range of souvenir, gift and Australiana-style shops.
- ✉ Between Hay Street Mall and St George's Terrace, Perth

☎ (08) 9325 4665
🚍 City Area Transit bus

New South Wales
Djamu Gallery
The Australian Museum has housed its indigenous gallery in Historic Customs House. An exhibition of art and craft.

✉ Customs House, Circular Quay, Sydney ☎ (02) 9320 6393
🚇 Circular Quay

Coo-ee Aboriginal Art
This interesting shop offers both Aboriginal artworks and authentic hand-made gifts and souvenirs.

✉ 98 Oxford Street, Paddington, Sydney
☎ (02) 9332 1544 🚍 380, L82

Queensland
Queensland Aboriginal Creations
This city store stocks Aboriginal items of all kinds – from didgeridoos to woodcarvings.

✉ 135 George Street, Brisbane
☎ (07) 3224 5730
🚍 City Circle 333

Victoria
Aboriginal Desert Art Gallery
A fine gallery selling a wide variety of Aboriginal artworks, particularly from the Central Desert region.

✉ 31 Flinders Lane, Melbourne
☎ (03) 9654 2516
🚍 City Circle tram

Tasmania
Tiagarra Aboriginal Culture and Art Centre
An excellent Aboriginal center and museum which also sells good quality arts and crafts.

✉ Mersey Bluff, Bluff Road, Devonport

☎ (03) 6424 8250 🚍 None

South Australia
Gallerie Australis
This highly recommended outlet in Adelaide's top hotel sells high quality Aboriginal arts, crafts and artefacts.

✉ Lower Forecourt Plaza, Hyatt Regency Adelaide, North Terrace, Adelaide
☎ (08) 8231 4111
🚍 City Loop or 99B

Tandanya Aboriginal Cultural Institute
This center's gift shop is stocked with well-made Aboriginal artworks and artefacts.

✉ 253 Grenfell Street, Adelaide ☎ (08) 8223 2467
🚍 City Loop

Northern Territory
Framed
Featuring Aboriginal art, crafts, sculptures and gifts, this Darwin gallery is very much worth visiting.

✉ 55 Stuart Highway, Stuart Park, Darwin
☎ (08) 8981 2994 🚍 None

The Original Dreamtime Gallery
At this large gallery you can buy Aboriginal themed clothing and jewelry, as well as carvings, pottery and other artifacts.

✉ 63 Todd Mall, Alice Springs
☎ (08) 8952 8861; fax (08) 8953 2803 🚍 None

Western Australia
Creative Native
One of Perth's best Aboriginal art centers, with everything from paintings to silk scarves and jewelry.

✉ 32 King Street, Perth
☎ (08) 9322 3398
🚍 City Area Transit bus

Australian Made!
International products and labels are well represented, but there are some uniquely Australian purchases that are particularly appealing. Beachwear and designer T-shirts, such as those created by Ken Done, are colorful and innovative, while Aussie 'bush clothing' is also popular. Other Australiana includes unusual Aboriginal-designed clothing and crafts, and home-grown products such as sheepskin items, designer knitwear, opals and South Sea pearls.

Jewelry, Stores & Shopping Centers

Opals, diamonds and pearls

Australia produces most of the world's opals, and Australian stones are considered to be of a particularly fine quality. You can buy either 'white', or the more expensive 'black' opals, unset or made up into beautiful jewelry. Other exclusive (and expensive) precious stone purchases – both from the north of Western Australia – are Argyle diamonds, available in white, champagne and pink varieties, and exquisite South Sea pearls.

Opals, Gems & Jewelry

New South Wales
Flame Opals
One of Sydney's best opal stockists offers a good range of stones, both unset and made up into fine jewelry.
✉ **119 George Street, The Rocks, Sydney** ☎ **(02) 9247 3446** 🚇 **Circular Quay**

Hardy Brothers
This gem specialist sells fine opals, South Sea pearls and Argyle diamonds from Western Australia, as well as other precious items.
✉ **Skygarden, 77 Castlereagh Street, Sydney** ☎ **(02) 9232 2422** 🚇 **St James**

Percy Marks Fine Gems
One of Sydney's oldest gem specialists, this store offers opals, Argyle diamonds and South Sea Pearls – all set in Australian hand-crafted jewelry.
✉ **60 Elizabeth Street, Sydney** ☎ **(02) 9233 1355** 🚇 **Martin Place**

Queensland
Quilpie Opals
This leading opal specialist sells beautiful stones direct from its Queensland mines.
✉ **Lennons Plaza, 68 Queen Street, Brisbane** ☎ **(07) 3221 7369** 🚌 **City Circle 333**

Victoria
Ashley Opals
This is one of the best places in Melbourne to buy opals, South Sea pearls and Argyle diamonds.
✉ **85 Collins Street, Melbourne** ☎ **(03) 9654 4866; fax (03) 9654 4889** 🚋 **City Circle tram**

Johnston Opals
Opals and opal-set jewelry are a specialty of this long-established company.
✉ **124 Exhibition Street, Melbourne** ☎ **(03) 9650 7434** 🚋 **City Circle tram**

Makers Mark Gallery
An upmarket outlet for beautifully crafted jewelry that incorporates exquisite Argyle diamonds and gems.
✉ **101 Collins Street, Melbourne** ☎ **(03) 9654 8488** 🚋 **City Circle Tram**

Tasmania
Handmark Gallery
Find innovative hand-made jewelry at this classy Hobart gallery.
✉ **77 Salamanca Place, Hobart** ☎ **(03) 6223 7895** 🚌 **None**

South Australia
The Opal Mine
South Australia produces 60 per cent of the world's opals, and this Adelaide outlet offers good-quality stones.
✉ **30 Gawler Place, Adelaide** ☎ **(08) 8223 4023; fax (08) 8223 2807** 🚌 **City Loop**

Northern Territory
Paspaley Pearls
Northern Australian pearls – regarded as the world's finest – and other exquisite jewelry are sold here.
✉ **Corner Bennett Street and The Mall, Darwin** ☎ **(08) 8981 9332** 🚌 **None**

Western Australia
Perth Mint
This museum of gold and minting has a shop that sells exclusive jewelry and gifts.
✉ **Corner Hay and Hill Streets, Perth** ☎ **(08) 9421 7277** 🚌 **City Area Transit bus**

Department Stores & Shopping Centers

New South Wales

David Jones
One of Australia's very best stores, glamorous 'DJs' operates from two enormous city center buildings.
✉ Elizabeth Street and Market Street, Sydney ☎ (02) 9266 5544 🚇 St James

Queen Victoria Building
This vast 1890s building, with its stained glass and floor tiling, is a delightful place in which to shop. There are over 200 boutiques here.
✉ Corner George, York and Market Streets, Sydney ☎ (02) 9264 9209 🚇 Town Hall

Australian Capital Territory

Canberra Centre
This three-level shopping center is Canberra's biggest – it contains a branch of David Jones and other large stores.
✉ Bunda Street, Canberra City ☎ (02) 6247 5611 🚌 301

Queensland

Marina Mirage
A waterfront Gold Coast shopping center which offers 80 speciality stores, boutiques and art galleries.
✉ Seaworld Drive, Broadwater Spit, Main Beach, Gold Coast ☎ (07) 5577 0088 🚌 1, 1A

Victoria

The Block Arcade
Opened in 1892, this historic arcade contains 30 shops and has a traditional European atmosphere.
✉ Between 282 Collins Street and 100 Elizabeth Street, Melbourne ☎ (03) 9654 5244 🚊 City Circle tram

Melbourne Central
This vast complex includes the international Daimaru Department Store and over 150 other specialty shops.
✉ 300 Lonsdale Street, Melbourne ☎ (03) 9665 0000 🚊 City Circle tram

Tasmania

Salamanca Place
This street's old sandstone warehouses have been converted into a delightful shopping complex offering arts, crafts, woolen goods and souvenirs.
✉ Salamanca Place, Hobart 🚌 None

South Australia

Rundle Mall
Adelaide's pedestrian mall is home to many shops and the city's major department stores.
✉ Rundle Mall, Adelaide 🚌 City Loop or 99B

Northern Territory

Smith Street Mall
Darwin's main shopping area offers everything from clothing stores to Aboriginal art galleries.
✉ Smith Street Mall, Darwin 🚌 None

Western Australia

Forrest Chase Shopping Plaza
This large, modern shopping center is one of the best places to shop in Perth. Convenient for the station.
✉ Murray Street, between Forrest Place and Barrack Street 🚌 City Area Transit bus

Duty- and Tax-free
Australia's duty- and tax-free prices are very competitive and compare favorably with those of Asian ports. Overseas visitors receive a discount of around 30 per cent on perfumes, cigarettes and alcohol, electrical and electronic equipment, jewelry, watches and other items. There are many duty-free shops in city centers and at the airports, and Australia even offers a facility for visitors to purchase duty-free goods on arrival at international airport terminals.

Markets

Out of Town

Although the best shopping is generally found in the center of capital cities, many suburbs, and even regional towns, offer some fine shops. City suburbs that are particularly good for shopping include Sydney's Paddington (offbeat fashions) and Double Bay (expensive designer clothing), and Melbourne's South Yarra and Toorak. Country town shopping – particularly for antiques and crafts – is excellent in NSW's Blue Mountains and Southern Highlands.

New South Wales

Paddington Bazaar

This Saturday market is the best in Sydney. There are over 250 stalls selling clothes and arts and crafts, as well as good food and free entertainment.

✉ **Corner Oxford and Newcombe Streets, Paddington, Sydney**
☎ **(02) 9331 2646** 🚌 **380, L82**

The Rocks Market

A lively Saturday and Sunday event in the heart of Sydney's tourist mecca.

✉ **Upper George Street, The Rocks, Sydney**
☎ **(02) 9255 1717**
🚊 **Circular Quay**

Australian Capital Territory

Old Bus Depot Markets

On Sundays, this old Canberra bus depot is transformed into an undercover market. Hand-made goods and collectables are the main items.

✉ **49 Wentworth Avenue, Kingston, Canberra**
☎ **(02) 6292 8391**
🕐 **Sun 10–4** 🚌 **313, 360**

Queensland

Riverside Markets

A Sunday city-center market offering books, household wares, clothing and much more.

✉ **Riverside Centre and Eagle Street Pier, Eagle Street, Brisbane** 🚌 **City Circle 333**

Victoria

Queen Victoria Market

This Melbourne institution is a large indoor market selling everything from foodstuffs to fashion clothing.

✉ **Corner Elizabeth and Victoria Streets, Melbourne**

☎ **(03) 9658 9600**
🕐 **Daily except Mon & Wed**
🚊 **City Circle tram, then 50, 57 or 59**

St Kilda Esplanade Art & Craft Market

This popular Sunday market offers over 200 stalls that sell only hand-crafted items.

✉ **The Esplanade, St Kilda, Melbourne** 🚊 **any St Kilda tram**

Tasmania

Salamanca Market

This is the place to be in Hobart on Saturdays – an excellent market set against the historic backdrop of Salamanca Place.

✉ **Salamanca Place, Hobart**
☎ **(03) 6238 2843** 🚌 **None**

South Australia

Central Markets

Dating from 1870, this is mainly a produce market – but a fascinating place to wander around nonetheless.

✉ **Grote and Gouger Streets, Adelaide** ☎ **(08) 8203 7494**
🕐 **Tue, Thu–Sat. Closed public holidays** 🚌 **City Loop or 99B**

Northern Territory

Mindil Beach Sunset Markets

This evening market features arts and crafts, many tempting food stalls and free entertainment.

✉ **Mindil Beach, Darwin**
☎ **(08) 8981 3454**
🕐 **Apr–Oct: Thu; May–Aug: Sun** 🚌 **None**

Western Australia

Fremantle Markets

A National Trust classified indoor market that sells fresh produce, clothing and crafts.

✉ **84 South Terrace, Fremantle**
☎ **(08) 9335 2515** 🕐 **Fri–Sun**
🚉 **Fremantle**

Crafts & Antiques

New South Wales
Australian Craftworks
Housed in a historic Sydney building, this is a collection of small shops selling high-quality arts and crafts.

✉ 127 George Street, The Rocks, Sydney
☎ (02) 9247 7156
🚉 Circular Quay

Peppergreen in Berrima
The Southern Highlands region is packed with antiques shops, but this large establishment offers an outstanding range of goods.

✉ Market Place, Berrima
☎ (02) 4877 1488
🚌 None

Sydney Antique Centre
This large center contains some 60 shops on two floors. The antiques range from jewelry to clocks, figurines, books and dolls.

✉ 531 South Dowling Street, Surry Hills, Sydney
☎ (02) 9361 324
🚌 378, 380

Australian Capital Territory
Cuppacumbalong Craft Centre
Located in a charming old homestead, this center is the outlet for painters, potters, weavers and other craftspeople.

✉ Naas Road, Tharwa
☎ (02) 6237 5116 🚌 None

Queensland
Paddington Antique Centre
A good range of antiques is available here, just 3km west of Brisbane's city center.

✉ 167 Latrobe Terrace, Paddington, Brisbane
☎ (07) 3369 8458
🚌 144, 362

Victoria
Convent Gallery
This magnificently restored former nunnery is now home to fine art, sculpture, jewelry, food and wine.

✉ Cnr Hill and Daly Streets, Daylesford
☎ (03) 5348 3211 🚌 none

Potoroo
Award-winning Melbourne outlet sells fine art and craftworks, including unusual ceramics and glassware.

✉ Southgate, Southbank, Melbourne ☎ (03) 9690 9859
🚋 City Circle tram

Tasmania
Saddlers Court
The historic village of Richmond, just 30 minutes' drive from Hobart, is full of crafts and antiques outlets, including this interesting collection of shops.

✉ 48–50 Bridge Street, Richmond ☎ (03) 6260 2132
🚌 Tiger Line from Hobart

South Australia
The Jam Factory Craft and Design Centre
This old Adelaide food factory is an excellent place to find South Australian designed jewelry, and crafts such as ceramics and leather goods.

✉ 19 Morphett Street (corner with North Terrace), Adelaide
☎ (08) 8410 0727
🚌 City Loop or 99B

Western Australia
Fremantle Arts Centre
An excellent Fremantle art gallery, which also sells a good selection of high-quality local arts and crafts.

✉ 1 Finnerty Street, Fremantle
☎ (08) 9335 8244
🚌 Fremantle

Shopping Tours
Shopping is such big business in Australia (many visitors come with this activity very much in mind) that organized tours – usually concentrating on discounted factory and warehouse shopping – are common in the large cities. In Sydney you can join Shopping Spree (☎ 02 9360 6220), Melbourne offers the similarly named Shopping Spree Tours (☎ 03 9596 6600), while in South Australia, Adelaide Shopping Tours (☎ 08 8234 2400) provide expert local knowledge.

Thrill Rides, Animal Parks & Fun Tours

Theme Parks

Children are exceptionally well catered for in Australia, with a wide range of museums, wildlife parks and other engrossing amusements. The theme parks are particularly good, including everything from the historical re-creations of Sovereign Hill in Victoria and Old Sydney Town, to the Gold Coast's educational Sea World and its entertainment complexes of Dreamworld, Wet 'n' Wild Water World and Warner Bros Movie World.

New South Wales

Australia's Wonderland

Incorporating thrilling rides, displays, shows and an excellent wildlife park, this suburban Sydney theme park is Australia's largest. Should appeal to all the family.
⊠ **Wallgrove Road, Eastern Creek, Sydney** ☎ **1800 252 198**
🕐 **Australia's Wonderland: weekends & school / public hols 10–5. Australian Wildlife Park: daily 9–5. Both closed 25 Dec**
🚉 **Rooty Hill, then bus**

Bounty Cruises

People of all ages will have fun sailing Sydney Harbour on this faithful re-creation of the famous 18th-century ship, HMAV *Bounty*.
⊠ **From Campbells Cove, The Rocks, Sydney**
☎ **(02) 9247 1789** 🕐 **Daily cruises** 🚉 **Circular Quay**

Old Sydney Town

On the Central Coast, an hour from the city, this re-creation of life in Sydney 200 years ago makes for an entertaining day out.
⊠ **Pacific Highway, Somersby**
☎ **(02) 4340 1104**
🕐 **Wed–Sun (& daily during school holidays) 10–4**
🚉 **Gosford, then bus**

Australian Capital Territory

Australian Institute of Sport

Sports-loving children will enjoy a tour of this national training center and its excellent facilities. Tours are led by some of Australia's elite athletes.
⊠ **Leverrier Crescent, Bruce (Belconnen)** ☎ **(02) 6214 1111 or (02) 6252 1444**
🕐 **Mon–Fri 9–5, Sat–Sun & public hols 10–4** 🚌 **431**

Queensland

Australian Woolshed

Just 20 minutes from Brisbane, you can watch sheep and sheepdog shows and visit the wildlife park.
⊠ **148 Samford Road, Ferny Hills, Brisbane**
☎ **(07) 3351 5366**
🕐 **Daily 9–5** 🚉 **Ferny Grove**

Lone Pine Koala Sanctuary

Close to Brisbane city, this sanctuary specializes in koalas but also contains kangaroos, wombats and other Australian animals.
⊠ **Jesmond Road, Fig Tree Pocket, Brisbane**
☎ **(07) 3378 1366** 🕐 **Daily 8–5**
🚤 **Lone Pine Koala Sanctuary (river boat from city center)**

Tjapukai Aboriginal Cultural Park

North of Cairns, this exciting and educational complex includes dance shows, boomerang throwing, an Aboriginal camp and other aspects of indigenous culture.
⊠ **Captain Cook Highway, Smithfield, Cairns**
☎ **(07) 4042 9900** 🕐 **Daily 9–5**
🚌 **Marlin Coast Sun Bus**

Victoria

Healesville Sanctuary

There are over 200 species of Australian animals at this natural bushland sanctuary, just an hour from Melbourne.
⊠ **Badger Creek Road, Healesville** ☎ **(03) 5962 4022**
🕐 **Daily 9–5** 🚉 **None**

Scienceworks

A suburban Melbourne museum with fun, hands-on exhibits, live science shows and technological activities
⊠ **2 Booker Street, Spotswood, Melbourne**

📷 (03) 9392 4800
🕐 Daily 10–4:30. Closed Good
Fri, 25 Dec 🚌 Spotswood

Tasmania
Bonorong Park Wildlife Centre
An award-winning wildlife park near Hobart, where you can meet Tasmanian devils, wombats, koalas, kangaroos and other native Australian animals.
✉️ Briggs Road, Brighton
📷 (03) 6268 1184
🕐 Daily 9–5. Closed 25 Dec
🚌 Tiger Line bus from Hobart

Cadbury-Schweppes Chocolate Factory
Taking children on a tour of this tempting attraction near Hobart may be asking for trouble, but it's a fun experience! Bookings are essential and children must have adult supervision.
✉️ Cadbury Road, Claremont, Hobart 📷 (03) 6249 0333
🕐 Mon–Fri: tours at 9, 9:30, 10:30, 11:15 & 1. Closed all public hols
🚢 Cruise from Hobart

South Australia
Glenelg
Taking a tram to this seaside Adelaide suburb is great fun, and once there kids can enjoy the beach and the Magic Mountain fun fair.
✉️ Magic Mountain, Colley Reserve, Glenelg, Adelaide
📷 (08) 8294 8199 🕐 Mon–Fri 9AM–10PM, Sat-Sun 12:30 –midnight 🚋 Glenelg tram

South Australian Maritime Museum
This fascinating museum will appeal to older children. There are moored vessels, interior exhibits and even a lighthouse.

✉️ 126 Lipson Street, Port Adelaide 📷 (08) 8240 0200
🕐 Daily 10–5. Closed 25 Dec
🚌 Port Adelaide

Northern Territory
Aquascene
Every day at high tide, thousands of fish come here to be hand fed – an experience that should appeal to children.
✉️ 28 Doctors Gully Road, Darwin 📷 (08) 8981 7837
🕐 Daily. Feeding times depend on tides 🚌 None

Frontier Camel Tours
This operation offers both short and long rides from its camel farm. There is also a camel museum and a reptile house.
✉️ Ross Highway, Alice Springs 📷 (08) 8953 0444
🕐 Daily 9–5 🚌 None

Western Australia
Rottnest Island
A day trip from Perth to this lovely island (► 89) is recommended. Children will enjoy the sandy beaches, clear waters and cute quokkas – small marsupials that roam the island.
✉️ Rottnest Island Visitor Centre, Thomson Bay
📷 (08) 9372 9752 🕐 Daily 8–5
🚢 Rottnest Island

Underwater World
With its dolphin pool, sharks and examples of over 200 marine species, this aquarium in Perth's northern suburbs is a fun and educational destination.
✉️ Hillary's Boat Harbour, West Coast Highway, Sorrento
📷 (08) 9447 7500 🕐 Daily 9–5. Closed 25 Dec 🚌 None

Outdoor Activities
Australia's Great Outdoors offers endless entertainment for youngsters. There are wonderful beaches to enjoy, national parks to explore, and outdoor activities such as horse riding. Most kids will also love the 'meet the sea creatures' events at Monkey Mia in Western Australia (dolphins), and in Darwin (hand feeding fish).

Theater & Classical Entertainment

All Tastes Catered For

'Entertainment' in Australia covers everything from highbrow opera to high-spirited pubs and sporting activities of every kind. Most of the more cultural events are focused on the capital cities, but larger country towns, especially in New South Wales and Victoria, can offer surprisingly good theater. Australians have a great love of gambling and there is now a casino in each main city.

New South Wales
Capitol Theatre

Sydney has many theaters, but this delightfully restored old building is the city's most charming. Major musicals are often performed here.

✉ **13 Campbell Street, Haymarket, Sydney**
☎ **(02) 9266 4800**
🚇 **Central or Town Hall**

Sydney Opera House

It's not just opera that is performed here – the building includes venues for ballet, dance, classical music concerts and theater.

✉ **Bennelong Point, Sydney**
☎ **(02) 9250 7777; (02) 9250 7250 for tours** 🚇 **Circular Quay**

Australian Capital Territory
Canberra Theatre Centre

This is Canberra's main arts venue, where opera, ballet and theatrical shows are performed regularly.

✉ **Civic Square, London Circuit, Canberra City**
☎ **(02) 6257 1077; 1800 802 025 for information on National Festival of Australian Theatre**
🚌 **301**

Queensland
Queensland Performing Arts Complex

This large complex contains theaters and a concert hall, which host dance, theater and orchestral events.

✉ **Queensland Cultural Centre, South Bank, Brisbane**
☎ **(07) 3846 4646 for re-servations** 🚉 **South Brisbane**

Victoria
Princess Theatre

This ornate 1887 city theater is an atmospheric venue for plays and various other performances.

✉ **163 Spring Street, Melbourne** ☎ **(03) 9662 2911**
🚋 **City Circle tram**

Victorian Arts Centre

Melbourne's acclaimed arts center hosts performances by the major Australian opera and dance companies and symphony orchestras.

✉ **100 St Kilda Road, Melbourne** ☎ **(03) 9281 8000**
🚋 **Tram 1, 3, 5**

Tasmania
Theatre Royal

This charming 1830s theater – Australia's oldest – is still used for plays and other performances.

✉ **29 Campbell Street, Hobart**
☎ **(03) 6234 6266** 🚌 **None**

South Australia
Adelaide Festival Centre

With its concert hall and theaters, this modern complex is Adelaide's premier performing arts venue.

✉ **King William Road, Adelaide** ☎ **(08) 8216 8600**
🚌 **City Loop or 99B**

Northern Territory
Performing Arts Centre

This large complex is the home of Darwin's concert, dance and theater scene.

✉ **93 Mitchell Street, Darwin**
☎ **(08) 8981 1222** 🚌 **None**

Western Australia
His Majesty's Theatre

This charming early 1900s venue is the home of Perth theater and opera.

✉ **825 Hay Street, Perth**
☎ **(08) 9322 2929**
🚌 **City Area Transit bus**
❓ **Friends of the Theatre provide free theater tours daily 10–4**

Nightclubs & Casinos

New South Wales
Star City Casino
Sydney's new casino complex near Darling Harbour operates 24 hours a day.
- ✉ **80 Pyrmont Street, Pyrmont,**
- ☎ **(02)1800 700 700**
- 🕐 **Day & night** 🚆 **Light Rail**

Riva
This sophisticated hotel nightclub, offering both live and disco music, is one of Sydney's best.
- ✉ **Sheraton on the Park, 138 Castlereagh Street, Sydney**
- ☎ **(02) 9286 6666**
- 🕐 **Wed–Sat** 🚇 **St James**

Australian Capital Territory
Casino Canberra
You don't have to be into gambling, as this small boutique-style casino has restaurants, bars and one of Canberra's liveliest nightclubs.
- ✉ **21 Binara Street, Canberra City** ☎ **(02) 6257 7074**
- 🕐 **Daily noon–6AM** 🚌 **301**

Queensland
Conrad Jupiters Casino
The brash Gold Coast is the perfect venue for this glitzy casino complex, which offers a variety of entertainment.
- ✉ **Gold Coast Highway, Broadbeach, Gold Coast**
- ☎ **(07) 5592 8130**
- 🕐 **Daily** 🚌 **1, 1A**

Friday's Nightclub & Bar
With a great view of the river, this large Brisbane nightclub has everything. There are several restaurants, three bars, a few dance floors and live bands appearing regularly.
- ✉ **Riverside Centre, 123 Eagle Street, Brisbane**
- ☎ **(07) 3832 2122** 🕐 **Daily**
- 🚌 **City Circle 333**

Victoria
Joy, Melbourne Metro Nightclub
Here you will find progressive house and up-front dance music.
- ✉ **20–30 Bourke Street, Melbourne**
- ☎ **(03) 9663 4288**
- 🚊 **City Circle tram**

Tasmania
Wrest Point Casino
Much more than a casino, Tasmania's premier nightspot offers dining, bars, live music and the popular Regines Nightclub.
- ✉ **410 Sandy Bay Road, Sandy Bay, Hobart** ☎ **(03) 6225 0112**
- 🕐 **Daily** 🚌 **None**

South Australia
Adelaide Casino
This is worth visiting as much for the splendid architecture – a grand 1920s Adelaide railway station – as for its entertainment.
- ✉ **North Terrace, Adelaide**
- ☎ **(08) 8212 2811** 🕐 **Daily from 10AM. Closed Good Fri, 25 Dec** 🚌 **City Loop or 99B**

Northern Territory
MGM Grand Casino
This large beachfront casino complex is Darwin's most popular nightlife venue.
- ✉ **Gilruth Avenue, The Gardens, Darwin**
- ☎ **(08) 8946 2666**
- 🕐 **Daily** 🚌 **None**

Western Australia
Margeaux's
A classy nightclub in one of Perth's best hotels; Margeaux's includes a bar and a disco.
- ✉ **Parmelia Hilton, Mill Street, Perth**
- ☎ **(08) 9322 3622** 🕐 **Daily**
- 🚌 **None**

What's On
The best way to find out about the entertainment scene in each capital city is to study the local newspaper. The *Sydney Morning Herald*, for example, includes entertainment information every day, but this paper's Friday *Metro* guide is a comprehensive look at what's on during the coming week. The major newspapers also include information on where to obtain tickets for concerts and other events.

Pubs, Bars & Live Music

The Movies

The movie scene is alive and well in Australia. You can see all the latest releases soon after they have opened in the northern hemisphere. Keep a look-out, too, for some of Australia's excellent home-grown movies – 1990s films like *Shine*, *Babe*, *Priscilla Queen of the Desert* and *Muriel's Wedding* took the movie world by storm. Check the various newspaper entertainment pages for full details of films and venues.

New South Wales

The Basement

An atmospheric club which specializes in live jazz, blues, funk and other music.

✉ 29 Reiby Place, Circular Quay, Sydney ☎ (02) 9251 2797 🕐 Daily 🚇 Circular Quay

Mercantile Hotel

One of Sydney's most character-filled pubs, with live Irish music and draught Guinness.

✉ 25 George Street, The Rocks, Sydney ☎ (02) 9247 3570 🕐 Daily 🚇 Circular Quay

Round Midnight

This intimate club is one of Sydney's best venues for drinking, dancing and listening to quality blues and jazz. It is open until very late most nights.

✉ 2 Roslyn Street, Kings Cross, Sydney ☎ (02) 9356 4045 🕐 Daily 🚇 Kings Cross

Australian Capital Territory

Gypsy Bar & Brasserie

Mix with the locals at this award-winning bar, well known for its live music.

✉ 9 East Row, Canberra City ☎ (02) 6247 7300 🕐 Daily until late, sometimes on Sun 🚌 307, 308

Queensland

Brisbane Centra

One of Brisbane's main jazz venues – top Australian and international musicians perform here each week.

✉ Roma Street, Brisbane ☎ (07) 3238 2222 🕐 Jazz Tue–Sat 🚉 Roma Street

Press Club

The city's newest and trendiest cafe and bar with a DJ playing cool music seven nights a week.

✉ Cnr Brunswick and Ann Sreets, Fortitude Valley ☎ (07) 3852 1216 🚌 322, 232, 476

Victoria

The Purple Emerald

This groovy and retro-style bar plays live jazz five nights a week, Wednesday to Sunday.

✉ 191 Flinders Lane, Melbourne ☎ (03) 9650 7753 🚋 City Circle tram

Tasmania

Nickelby's Wine Bar

This is the ideal place to sample fine Tasmanian wines and meet some Hobart locals.

✉ 217 Sandy Bay Road, Sandy Bay, Hobart ☎ (03) 6223 6030 🕐 Daily 🚌 Busy Bee bus

South Australia

The Cargo Club

A lively central Adelaide club; live jazz, soul and funk are a bonus on some nights.

✉ 213 Hindley Street, Adelaide ☎ (08) 8231 2327 🕐 Live music Thu and Sun 🚌 99B

Northern Territory

The Carlton Darwin

One of the best hotels in Darwin, with comfortable bars and live entertainment.

✉ The Esplanade, Darwin ☎ (08) 8982 9911 🕐 Daily 🚌 None

Western Australia

Metropolis Concert Club

This smart club is one of the Perth area's best venues for live music.

✉ 58 South Terrace, Fremantle ☎ (08) 9336 1880 🕐 Daily 9–5 🚉 Fremantle

Sports & Adventures

Ballooning

Balloon Aloft
Hot air ballooning is a great way to see Canberra's layout, while also enjoying an unusual adventure.
✉ Canberra, Australian Capital Territory
☎ (02) 6285 1540
🕐 Daily at dawn from various locations 🚌 None

Bushwalking

Tasmanian Expeditions
Tasmania's national parks and World Heritage areas are wonderful for bushwalking. Novices should join a guided tour as this is true wilderness.
✉ 110 George Street, Launceston, Tasmania
☎ (03) 6334 3477 🚌 None

Cricket and Australian Rules Football

Melbourne Cricket Ground
A visit to the famous Melbourne Cricket Ground is a must for sporting fans – cricket is played here in summer, and Australian Rules football in winter.
✉ Jolimont Terrace, Jolimont, Melbourne, Victoria
☎ (03) 9657 8888
🚌 Trams 48, 75

Adelaide Oval
Watch exciting summer cricket matches, and winter Australian Rules football games.
✉ King William Road, North Adelaide, South Australia
☎ (08) 8231 9701 🚌 None

Fishing
Darwin is the ideal departure point for game fishing, and many operators offer escorted trips – details are available from the local tourism association.
✉ Darwin Region Tourism Assocation, 33 Smith Street Mall, Darwin, Northern Territory
☎ (08) 8981 4300 🚌 None

Golf

Palm Meadows
There are so many top quality golf courses around the Gold Coast that the area could well be renamed the 'Golf Coast'. One of the best is the course at Palm Meadows.
✉ Palm Meadows Drive, Carrara, Gold Coast, Queensland
☎ (07) 5594 2450
🕐 Daily 🚌 1, 1A

Burswood Resort Golf Course
There are some fine golf courses around Perth; one of the best is at the Burswood Island Resort.
✉ Great Eastern Highway, Victoria Park, Perth, Western Australia ☎ (08) 9362 7576
🕐 Daily 🚌 None

Skiing
Winter sports fans who are visiting during the ski season should sample a ski field.
✉ Thredbo Village, New South Wales ☎ 1800 020 589
🕐 Daily from mid-Jun–early Oct ❎ Cooma, then a bus

Swimming

North Sydney Olympic Pool
A swim at this harborside pool (open air in summer) is a great experience.
✉ North Sydney Olympic Pool, Alfred Street, Milsons Point, Sydney ☎ (02) 9955 2309
🕐 Mon–Fri 6AM–9PM, Sat–Sun 7–7 🚉 Milsons Point

Outdoor Entertainment
Australia's climate lends itself to outdoor entertainment, and there are many alfresco events for visitors to enjoy. In Melbourne, regular events take place at the Myer Music Bowl; in Sydney, January brings open-air opera and classical music concerts in the Domain; while Darwin offers 'Sunset Jazz' each Sunday from April to September. There are also free concerts in public spaces and parkland throughout the nation in the summer months.

What's On When

Gay and Lesbian Mardi Gras

Australia's most colorful and well-attended festival is Sydney's Gay and Lesbian Mardi Gras. The festival's spectacular street parade, staged in late February or early March, has grown from humble beginnings in 1978 to attract around 700,000 spectators and some 6,000 participants each year.

As a nation, Australia spends a considerable amount of time in holiday and party mode. There are nine annual national public holidays, and each state holds at least one major festival each year. These range from the highbrow artistic and cultural events of the Adelaide, Melbourne and Sydney festivals to sporting carnivals and such downright bizarre happenings as the waterless Alice Springs Henley-on-Todd Regatta.

January

Mid- to late Jan – Ford Australian Open (tennis, Melbourne).
26 – Australia Day holiday and celebrations.
All month – Sydney Festival.

February

Variable – Chinese New Year Festival (around Australia).
All month – Sydney Gay and Lesbian Mardi Gras (▶ panel).
Feb/Mar – Adelaide Festival and Adelaide Fringe Festival (even-numbered years only).
Mid-Feb to early Mar – Festival of Perth.

March

First two weeks – Moomba Festival (Melbourne).
Early Mar – Australian Formula One Grand Prix (motor racing, Melbourne).
Early to mid-Mar – Canberra Festival.
Late Mar to early Apr – Barossa Valley Vintage Festival (odd-numbered years only); Royal Easter Show (Sydney).

April

25 – Anzac Day holiday.

May

Early May – Bangtail Muster (parade, Alice Springs).

Late May to early Jun – Biennial festival of Music (Brisbane, odd-numbered years only).

June

Wintersun Festival (Gold Coast).

July

Mid-Jul – Lions Camel Cup (camel races, Alice Springs).
All month – Darwin Cup Carnival (horse racing).
Late July – Royal Darwin Show.

August

Early or mid-Aug – City to Surf fun run (Sydney).
Mid- to late Aug – Festival of Darwin.
Late Aug – Alice Springs Rodeo.

September

Late Sep – AFL Grand Final (Australian Rules football, Melbourne).
Mid -Sep to early Oct – Floriade Spring Festival (Canberra).

October

Early Oct – Indy Carnival (motor racing, Gold Coast); Henley-on-Todd Regatta (Alice Springs); Manly International Jazz Festival (Sydney).
Mid-Oct – Reef Festival of Cairns.
Mid-Oct to early Nov – Melbourne International Festival of the Arts.

November

First Tue – Melbourne Cup horse race.
Late Nov – Fremantle Festival.

December

Late Dec to early Jan – Hobart Summer Festival.

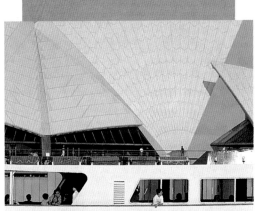

CAPTAIN COOK CRUISES

Practical Matters

Before You Go   118
When You Are There   119–123
Language   124

Above: *Captain Cook Cruises, Sydney*
Right: *Totem pole at the Australian Museum, Sydney*

WHAT YOU NEED

- ● Required
- ○ Suggested
- ▲ Not required

	UK	Germany	USA	Netherlands	Spain
Passport (valid for six months from date of entry)	●	●	●	●	●
Visa	●	●	●	●	●
Onward or Return Ticket	●	●	●	●	●
Health Inoculations	▲	▲	▲	▲	▲
Health Documentation (reciprocal agreement document) (▶ 123, Health)	●	▲	▲	●	▲
Travel Insurance	●	●	●	●	●
Driving License (national) and International Driving Permit	●	●	●	●	●

WHEN TO GO

Australia (Sydney)

| ▮ High season |
| ▯ Low season |

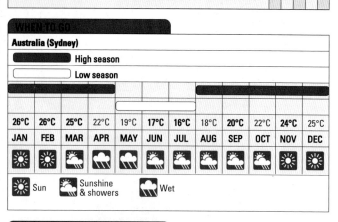

JAN	FEB	MAR	APR	MAY	JUN	JUL	AUG	SEP	OCT	NOV	DEC
26°C	26°C	25°C	22°C	19°C	17°C	16°C	18°C	20°C	22°C	24°C	25°C

☀ Sun   ⛅ Sunshine & showers   🌧 Wet

TOURIST OFFICES

In the UK
Australian Tourist
Commission
Gemini House,
10-18 Putney Hill
London SW15 6AA
☎ 020 8780 2229
Fax: 020 8780 1496

In the USA
Australian Tourist
Commission
2049 Century Park East
Suite 1920
Los Angeles CA 90067
☎ 310/229 4870
Fax: 310/552 1215

WHEN YOU ARE THERE

ARRIVING

All major airlines operate services to Australia. Qantas, the Australian national airline, flies from London to Australia's international airports.
Flights from Europe take between 20 and 30 hours; flights from North America take about 15 hours.

Sydney Airport Kilometers to city center	**Journey times**	
		N/A
10 kilometers		35 minutes
		35 minutes

Darwin Airport Kilometers to city center	**Journey times**	
		N/A
12.5 kilometers		15 minutes
		15 minutes

MONEY

The monetary unit of Australia is the Australian dollar ($A) and cents (100 cents = 1 $A dollar).

Coins come in 5¢, 10¢, 20¢, 50¢ and $1 and $2 denominations, and there are $5, $10, $20, $50 and $100 notes.

Major credit cards are accepted in all large cities and most airports and banks have facilities for changing foreign currency and traveler's checks.

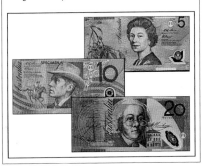

TIME

 Australia has three time zones. Perth (WA) is 8 hours ahead of GMT (GMT+8) and Sydney (NSW) is 10 hours ahead of GMT (GMT+10). Daylight Saving Time varies from state to state.

CUSTOMS

 YES

Airports have inbound duty-free stores. There are duty-free allowances for those over 18 years of age.
Alcohol: spirits: 1.125L
Cigarettes: 250 or
Tobacco: 250gm
Perfume or toilet water: no limit but a duty/tax free allowance of $A400 per person over 18 and $A200 per person under 18 is available for goods intended as gifts. These articles must accompany you through customs and must not be intended for commercial purposes.
There are no restrictions on the import or export of Australian currency although a report form must be completed for amounts over $A5,000.

 NO

Drugs, steroids, weapons, firearms, protected wildlife and associated products. There are very strict regulations governing the importation of foods, plants and animals.

TOURIST OFFICES

Australian Capital Territory
- ACT Visitor Information
Centre
Northbourne Ave,
Dixon 2602
☎ (02) 6205 0044

New South Wales
- NSW Travel Centre
19 Castlereagh Street
Sydney 2000
☎ (02) 9231 4444

Queensland
- Queensland Travel Centre
243 Edward Street
Brisbane 4000
☎ (07) 3874 2800

Western Australia
- WA Tourist Centre
Forrest Place (nr
Wellington Street)
Perth 6000
☎ (08) 9483 1111

Northern Territory
- NT Holiday Centre
PO Box 2532,
Alice Springs, NT0871
☎ (08) 89 518 571

Tasmania
- Tasmanian Travel and
Information Centre
20 Davey Street
Hobart 7000
☎ (03) 62 30 8233

Even the smallest towns
have an outlet distributing
tourist information. Look for
the international 🄸 sign,
which may be displayed at
an information center,
community hall or service
station.

NATIONAL HOLIDAYS

J	F	M	A	M	J	J	A	S	O	N	D
2		(2)	(1/3)		1						2

1 Jan	New Year's Day
26 Jan (first Mon after)	Australia Day
Variable	Labour Day
Mar/Apr	Good Friday
Mar/Apr	Easter Monday
25 Apr	Anzac Day
9 Jun (or second Mon)	Queen's Birthday
25 Dec	Christmas Day
26 Dec	Boxing Day

In addition, individual states have public holidays
throughout the year for agricultural shows, e.g.
Brisbane Royal Show; regattas and race days, e.g.
Melbourne Cup Day.

OPENING HOURS

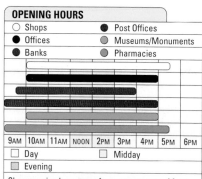

○ Shops	● Post Offices
● Offices	◐ Museums/Monuments
● Banks	◐ Pharmacies

9AM	10AM	11AM	NOON	2PM	3PM	4PM	5PM	6PM

☐ Day	☐ Midday
☐ Evening	

Shop opening hours vary from state to state. Many
supermarkets and department stores have late night
opening on Thursday or Friday until 8 or 9PM and are
open 9AM–5PM on Saturday. Shops in tourist centers
and pedestrianized areas in cities are often open on
Sunday. Some pharmacies are open longer hours
than shown above and offer a 24-hour service in big
cities. Opening times of museums may vary.

DRIVE ON THE
LEFT

TOILETS
FREE

PUBLIC TRANSPORT

 Internal Flights Australia has a dense network of domestic and regional air services. Many airlines offer outstanding discount deals, but check before departure whether you need to purchase tickets or passes before you go. Qantas and Ansett Australia are the main domestic airlines. Contact your travel agent for full details.

 Trains Most capital cities have frequent services between business districts and the suburbs. Long-distance trains offer sleeping berths and reclining seats, and most interstate trains have dining or buffet cars. Reservations are accepted up to nine months in advance on long-distance trains. Rail Australia ☎ (UK) 01733 335 599.

 Bus travel Excellent long-distance express bus services run daily between major cities, serviced by Greyhound Pioneer Australia (☎ 132 030) and McCafferty's Express Coaches (☎ 131 499). Coaches are non-smoking, have air-conditioning and on-board bathrooms. Tasmania is serviced by Tasmanian Redline Coaches.

 Ferries The only regular interstate ferry service is TT Line's passenger/vehicle ferry *Spirit of Tasmania*, between Melbourne and Devonport in Tasmania, departing Melbourne on Mon, Wed and Fri and returning on Tue, Thu and Sat. ☎ (Australia) (0364) 21 7333; Fax (0364) 24 4966.

 Urban Transport Most state capital cities have good train services and/or frequent bus services which operate between the city center and the suburbs. Perth and Sydney also have regular local ferry services, and trams run in the city centers of Melbourne, Adelaide and Sydney. Smoking is not permitted in most public vehicles.

CAR RENTAL

 Rental cars/ motorhomes are available at major air and rail terminals and from cities throughout Australia. It is advisable to book, especially during December and January. Most rental companies offer advice and provide relevant guides and maps.

TAXIS

 Except in some country towns, all taxis in Australia operate on a meter system. All fares are as displayed on the meter. Taxis can be booked (at an extra charge) or they can be stopped on the street. Smoking is not permitted in most public vehicles.

DRIVING

 Speed limit on freeways: **110kph**

Speed limit on all country roads: **100kph**

Speed limit on urban roads: **60kph**

 It is compulsory for drivers and passengers to wear seat belts at all times.

Random breath testing is carried out in most Australian states. Limit: 0.05% of alcohol in blood.

Petrol comes in leaded and unleaded grades and is sold by the liter. Service stations are plentiful, except in some Outback areas, but trading hours vary. Most service stations accept international credit cards.

 If your hire car breaks down you should contact the rental company, which will arrange to send road service to your location and repair the vehicle. Alternatively, most service stations will be able to assist or, at least, direct you to the nearest repair center. Check with your own motoring club regarding reciprocal facilities.

PERSONAL SAFETY

In crowded places, the usual safety precautions should be taken. Walking in the bush and swimming have their hazards.

- Hitch-hiking is not recommended: this is illegal in some states.
- Women should avoid walking alone at night.
- If bushwalking or camping, leave an itinerary with friends. Wear boots, socks and trousers.
- Take care and heed warning signs when swimming, whether in the sea or fresh water (crocodiles!)

Police assistance:
☎ **000**
from any phone

TELEPHONES

Long-distance calls within Australia (STD) and International Direct Dialing (IDD) can be made on public payphones (check with operator for charges). Public payphones accept cash and *Phonecard*, which is available from retail outlets in denominations of $A5, $A10, $A20 and $A50. The *Country Direct* service gives access to over 50 countries for collect or credit card calls. Phones that accept credit cards can be found at airports, central city locations and many hotels. *Telstra PhoneAway* prepaid card enables you to use virtually any phone in Australia with all call costs charged against the card.

International Dialing Codes

From Australia to:	
UK:	**0011 44**
Germany:	**0011 49**
USA:	**0011 1**
Netherlands:	**0011 31**
Spain:	**0011 34**

POST

Post Offices
The offices of Australia Post are located in city centers, the suburbs and are often combined with a general store in smaller places. Postal and *poste restante* services are available. Some mail boxes are traditional; most, painted red with a white stripe, resemble litter bins. Opening times 9–5 Mon–Fri.

ELECTRICITY

The power supply is: 240/250 volts, 50 cycles AC. Sockets accept three-flat-

pin plugs so you may need an adaptor. If your appliances are 110v check if there is a 110/240v switch; if not you will need a voltage converter. Universal outlets for 240v or 110v shavers are usually found in leading hotels.

TIPS/GRATUITIES

Yes ✓ No ✕		
Restaurants (service not incl)	✓	10%
Bar service	✕	
Taxis	✕	
Tour guides		optional
Hairdressers	✕	
Chambermaids	✕	
Porters (hotel) per bag	✓	$A1–2
Theater/cinema attendants	✕	
Cloakroom attendants	✕	
Toilets	✕	

HEALTH

Insurance
British and certain other nationals are eligible for free basic care at public hospitals but it is strongly recommended that all travelers take out a comprehensive medical insurance policy.

Dental Services
Dentists are plentiful and the standard of treatment is high – as are the bills. In an emergency go to the casualty wing of a local hospital, or locate a dentist from the local telephone book. Medical insurance is essential.

Sun Advice
The sun in Australia is extremely strong, especially in summer. Wear a hat to protect your face and neck and avoid sunbathing in the middle of the day. Use a high-factor sun screen.

Drugs
Prescription and non-prescription drugs are available from chemists or pharmacies. Visitors may import up to four weeks supply of prescribed medication: bring a doctor's certificate.

Safe Water
It is safe to drink tap water throughout Australia. Bottled mineral water is available throughout the country.

CONCESSIONS

Students/Youths Young visitors should join the International Youth Hostels Federation before leaving their own country. Australia has a widespread network of youth and backpacker hostels. International Student or Youth Identity Cards may entitle the holder to discounts on attractions.

Senior Citizens Many attractions offer a discount for senior citizens; the age limit varies from 60 to 65, and your passport should be sufficient evidence of age. However, few discounts on travel are available to overseas senior citizens, as an Australian pension card is usually required to qualify.

CLOTHING SIZES

Australia	UK	Europe		
36	36	46	36	
38	38	48	38	
40	40	50	40	Suits
42	42	52	42	
44	44	54	44	
46	46	56	46	
7	7	41	8	
7.5	7.5	42	8.5	
8.5	8.5	43	9.5	Shoes
9.5	9.5	44	10.5	
10.5	10.5	45	11.5	
11	11	46	12	
14.5	14.5	37	14.5	
15	15	38	15	
15.5	15.5	39/40	15.5	Shirts
16	16	41	16	
16.5	16.5	42	16.5	
17	17	43	17	
8	8	34	6	
10	10	36	8	
12	12	38	10	Dresses
14	14	40	12	
16	16	42	14	
18	18	44	16	
4.5	4.5	37.5	6	
5	5	38	6.5	
5.5	5.5	38.5	7	Shoes
6	6	39	7.5	
6.5	6.5	40	8	
7	7	41	8.5	

WHEN DEPARTING

- The airport departure tax when leaving Australia is incorporated into the price of your air ticket.
- Contact the airline at least 72 hours before departure to 'reconfirm' that you intend to be on the flight. If you don't you could lose your seat.
- Arrive at the airport at least 2 hours before your departure time to avoid getting 'bumped'.

LANGUAGE

The common language of Australia is English, but it has been adapted and modified to form 'Strine', a colorful and abbreviated version of the mother tongue. The rather nasal Australian accent is quite distinctive and is spoken without any real regional variation throughout the country. The vocabulary contains a number of words of Aboriginal origin (didgeridoo and kangaroo), but the real joy of 'Strine' is its slang. The following is a short list of words and abbreviations you may encounter.

Australian	English
ABC	Australian Broadcasting Corporation
ACT	Australian Capital Territory (Canberra Area)
ALP	Australian Labor Party
ANZAC	Australian and New Zealand Army Corps
arvo	afternoon
barbie	barbecue
bludger	scrounger
blue	a fight, or a redhead
bottle shop	off license/liquor store
bush	countryside
BYO	bring your own (drink to a restaurant)
cask	wine-box
chook	chicken
chunder	to vomit
cockie	farmer
crook	ill
drongo	slow-witted person
dunny	outside lavatory
esky	large insulated box for keeping beer etc cold
fossicking	hunting for precious stones
galah	a kind of parrot, an idiot
garbo	garbage collector
g'day	good day, traditional Australian greeting
interstate	anything to do with the other Australian states
jackaroo	young male trainee on a station (farm)
joey	baby kangaroo
lair, larriken	rogue, layabout, ruffian
lamington	a square of sponge cake covered in chocolate icing and coconut
lollies	sweets, candy
ocker	an Australian male with crude manners
ripper	good (also 'little ripper')
sandshoes	trainers, sneakers
semi-trailer	articulated truck
shoot through	to leave
snags	sausages
sprog	baby
station	large farm or ranch
strides	trousers
stubby	small bottle of beer
Tassie	Tasmania
tinny	can of beer
uni	university
unit	apartment, flat
ute	utility truck (pickup truck)
wowser	prude, killjoy
yakka	work

INDEX

Aboriginal people and culture
13, 16, 21, 22, 26, 73, 80,
104-5
accommodation 100-3
Adelaide 72-3, 76, 111
Adelaide Botanic Gardens 76
Adelaide Hills 77
Adelaide Zoo 76
Albany 88
Alice Springs 80
AMP Tower 34
Anglesea 20
animal parks 110, 111
Armadale 90
Arnhem Land 21
Art Gallery of New South Wales
36
Art Gallery of South Australia 73
Atherton Tableland 16
Australian Aviation Heritage
Centre 81
Australian Capital Territory
(ACT) 30, 42-3, 110
Australian Institute of Sport 110
Australian Museum 34
Australian National Botanic
Gardens 42
Australian Stockman's Hall of
Fame 53
Australian War Memorial 43
Ayers Rock see Uluru-Kata
Tjuta National Park

Ballarat 63
banks 120
Barossa Valley 77
Batchelor 81
Bathurst Island 69
Battery Point 66
Berrima 40
Berry Springs 81
Bicheno 66
Blackall Range 54
Blackheath 41
Blue Mountains 23, 41
Brisbane 48-9
Broken Hill 37
Broome 22
Bunbury 90
Bungle Bungles 22
buses 121
Byron Bay 37

Cairns 16, 55
Canberra 30, 42-3, 110
Carnarvon National Park 52
car rental 121
Cataract Gorge 66
Charters Towers 52
children's attractions 110-11
City Botanic Gardens, Brisbane
49
climate 118, 123
clothing sizes 123
Coffs Harbour 37
concessions 123

Coober Pedy 69
Coolgardie 88
Coonawarra region 69
Cradle Mountain-Lake St Clair
National Park 25
customs regulations 119

Daintree National Park 55
Dandenong Ranges 63
Darling Harbour 34
Darwin 79, 81
Darwin Botanic Gardens 79
Darwin Crocodile Farm 81
departure information 124
Devils Marbles 80
Dorrigo National Park 37
drives
Blue Mountains 41
Cairns to the Daintree 55
Darwin to Litchfield National
Park 81
South of Perth 90
driving 118, 121
duty- and tax-free prices 107

eating out 68, 92-9
electricity 122
embassies and consulates 120
emergency telephone numbers
119, 122
entertainment 112-16

fauna and flora 12-13
festivals and events 116
Flagstaff Hill Maritime Museum
20
Flinders Ranges 77
food and drink 44-5
Franklin-Gordon Wild Rivers
National Park 25, 67
Fraser Island 53
Fremantle 85
Freycinet Peninsula 66

Gammon Ranges National Park
16
Geikie Gorge National Park 22
geography 7
Glenelg 73
Gold Coast 17
Great Barrier Reef 7, 9, 18-19,
47
Great Ocean Road 20

Hartz Mountains National Park
25
health 118, 123
history 10-11
Hobart 65-6
Hunter Valley 38

internal flights 121

Jervis Bay 69

Kakadu National Park 13, 21
Kalgoorlie-Boulder 88
Kangaroo Island 77

Katherine 80
Kiama 37
the Kimberley 22
Kings Park 85
Koala Conservation Centre 63
Kosciuszko National Park 40
Kuranda 52

Lamington National Park 53
language 124
Launceston 66
Leura 41
Litchfield National Park 81
local ways 68
Longreach 53
Lord Howe Island 40
Lorne 20
Loxton 77

MacDonnell Ranges 80
Magnetic Island 54, 69
Mandurah 90
maps
Australia 28–9
New South Wales 38–9
Northern Territory 78
Queensland 50–1
South Australia 74–5
Sydney 32–3
Tasmania 64–5
Victoria 60–1
Western Australia 86–7
Margaret River 88-9
Maritime Museum of Tasmania
66
Marlin Coast 55
Melbourne 58-62, 110
Melbourne Cricket Ground 59
Melville Island 69
the Midlands 67
Mindil Beach 79
Minnamurra Rainforest Reserve
37
money 119
Mossman River Gorge 55
Mount Coot-tha 49
Mount Tomah Botanic Garden 41
Mount Victoria 41
Murray Riverlands 77
museums 120
Museum and Art Gallery of the
Northern Territory 79
Myall Lakes National Park 40

Nambung National Park 89
National Gallery of Australia 43
National Gallery of Victoria 59
National Maritime Museum 34
National Motor Museum 77
national holidays 120
national parks and reserves 12
New South Wales 30-43, 110
Ningaloo Reef 69
Nitmiluk National Park 80
Noosa Heads 54
Norman Lindsay Gallery and
Museum 41
Northern Territory 71, 78–81,111

Oatlands 67
Old Melbourne Gaol 59
Old Telegraph Station 80
opals 106
opening hours 120
Otway National Park 20
Outback Heritage Centre 53

Parliament House 43
passports and visas 118
Pemberton 89
personal safety 122
Perth 84-5
pharmacies 120
Phillip Island 63
The Pinnacles 89
police 122
population 7
Port Arthur 67
Port Campbell 20
Port Campbell National Park 20
Port Douglas 55
Port Fairy 20
postal services 120, 122
Powerhouse Museum 35
public transport 121

Queensland 46-55, 110-11
Queensland Cultural Centre 49
Questacon 43

Rialto Towers Observation
  Deck 59
Rockingham 90
The Rocks 35
Ross 67
Rottnest Island 89, 111
Royal Botanic Gardens,
  Melbourne 62
Royal Botanic Gardens, Sydney
  36
Royal Flying Doctor Service 22,
  37, 80, 88

Royal Tasmanian Botanical
  Gardens 66

St George's Terrace 85
St Kilda 60
Salamanca Place 66
Scienceworks 110-11
Seal Bay Conservation Park 77
Shark Bay Marine Park 89
Shipwreck Coast 20
shopping 104-9, 120
Snowy Mountains 40
South Australia 71, 72-7, 111
South Australian Maritime
  Museum 111
South Australian Museum 73
South Bank Parklands 49
Southern Highlands 40
Southwest National Park 25
sport and leisure 69, 115
states and territories 7
Stirling Range National Park
  88
Strahan 67
Sunshine Coast 54
Surfers Paradise 17
Sydney 31-6, 110
Sydney Harbour 9, 24
Sydney Harbour Bridge 24, 35
Sydney Opera House 9, 24

Tandanya Aboriginal Cultural
  Institute 73
Taronga Zoo 35
Tasman Peninsula 67
Tasmania 25, 57, 64-7, 111
Tasmanian Devil Park 67
Tasmanian Museum and Art
  Gallery 66
Tasmanian Wool Centre 67
taxis 121
telephones 122
theme parks 110

time 118, 119
tipping 122
Tjapukai Aboriginal Cultural Park
  52, 110
toilets 121
tourist offices 118, 120
Townsville 54
trains 121
travelling to Australia 119
Tuart Forest National Park 90

Uluru-Kata Tjuta National Park 9,
  26

Van Diemen's Land Folk
  Museum 66
Victoria 57, 58-63, 110-11

walks
  Adelaide 76
  Melbourne 62
  Sydney 36
Warrawong Sanctuary 77
Watarrka National Park 80
Wave Rock 89
Wentworth Falls 41
Western Australia 82-90, 111
Western Australian Botanic
  Garden 85
Western Australian Maritime
  Museum 85
Western Australian Museum 85
Western Plains Zoo 37
Whitsunday Islands 54
William Ricketts Sanctuary 63
Wilpena Pound 16
Wilsons Promontory National
  Park 63
wine, beer, spirits 38, 45, 77, 88
Wolfe Creek Crater 22
World Heritage areas 12

Yalgorup National Park 90

Acknowledgments
The Automobile Association wishes to thank the following photographers and libraries for their assistance in the preparation of this book.
AUSTRALIA POST 122b; AUSTRALIAN TOURIST COMMISSION F/cover (c) Sydney Opera House, 11, 15b, 18/9, 19, 27a, 36, 64a, 67, 68, 73, 76, 79; BRUCE COLEMAN COLLECTION 6a, 22, 25, 51, 81; IMAGES COLOUR LIBRARY F/cover (a) Ayers Rock; INTERNATIONAL PHOTOBANK 15a, 16, 20, 23, 70, 84; MARY EVANS PICTURE LIBRARY 10; MRI BANKERS' GUIDE TO FOREIGN CURRENCY 119; PICTURES COLOUR LIBRARY 53, 88/9; REX FEATURES I4; ROBERT HARDING PICTURE LIBRARY F/cover (b) Koala; SPECTRUM COLOUR LIBRARY 17, 21, 47, 50, 52, 55, 72, 122a; STOCK MARKET PHOTO AGENCY INC. 54; TOURISM VICTORIA 61; WORLD PICTURES B/cover Aboriginal art.
The remaining photographs are from the Association's own library (AA PHOTO LIBRARY) with contributions from
Adrian Baker 5b, 7, 8a, 8b, 12, 13, 26, 31b, 32, 33a, 34, 37, 42, 46, 48, 49, 59, 62, 64b, 65, 69, 71, 80, 82, 83, 85, 86, 87, 90, 91a; Paul Kenward 1, 2, 5a, 6b, 9a, 9b, 24, 27b, 30, 31a, 33b, 35, 39, 40, 41, 43, 44, 45a, 45b, 91b, 117a, 117b; Christine Osborne 56, 57, 58, 63, 75

Contributors
Copy editors: Audrey Horne, Penny Phenix Page Layout: Design 23 Verifier: Sheila Hawkins
Researcher (Practical Matters): Lesley Allard Indexer: Marie Lorimer Updater: Rod Ritchie